ISBN 0 948417 20 X

Printed by
GOSPEL TRACT PUBLICATIONS
411 Hillington Road, Glasgow G52 4BL, Scotland

DAVID REA

Compiled by Tom Rea

NOVEMBER 1987
Published by
GOSPEL TRACT PUBLICATIONS
411 Hillington Road, Glasgow G52 4BL, Scotland

Contents

David Rea

The Life and Labours
of David Rea, evangelist

Introduction

In introducing this work to my readers, I feel deeply conscious of my inability to do so in a way worthy of him who for so many years heralded the Gospel of our Lord Jesus Christ with such powerful results.

It has further devolved upon me to not only present for publication the subject matter which he had so carefully produced, but also to augment this with a supplementary record.

No doubt, had he lived, he would himself have finished the work with a detailed minuteness which it has been impossible for me to attain. The Lord has, however, enabled me to acquire most of the particulars of his notable Gospel campaigns from the time he ceased to write until his home-call.

It has, therefore, been necessary to produce the book in two Parts. Part 1, which covers pages 7 to 118, contains the subject matter of his manuscripts, to the text of which, with very few exceptions, I have strictly adhered, so that on these pages we have the actual story of his life and labours as written by himself.

The commencement of Part 2 will be found on

page 121, where I continue the report of his work, for some of the particulars of which I am indebted to a few friends who were closely associated with him in Gospel work during the last twenty years of his life.

My father was born at Balteagh, near Portadown, in the year 1845. He was married in 1868 at Portadown First Presbyterian Church, and was converted in 1869. On the 2nd of September, 1916, at the age of 71 years, he fell asleep in Jesus.

TOM REA.

Chapter 1

CONVERSION, 1869

I have often been asked to publish the story of my conversion, and I do so now with the hope that the Lord will be pleased to make it the means of blessing to many others of my fellow-travellers to eternity.

It took place in the year 1869, but it is ever fresh in my memory. I am sure I never can forget it, and throughout the countless ages of eternity I shall praise my blessed Lord and Saviour for His infinite love and grace to such a sinner as I. I was one of those who ran with awful rapidity in the paths of sin and shame; indeed, my body was almost worn out in Satan's hard service.

I had several narrow escapes from death. I sometimes shudder when I think how near Hell I was at times. Drink was one of my besetting sins, and often in the midst of my days and nights of revellings, death and eternity troubled me, but I was never thoroughly aroused until one Sunday afternoon in the month of January.

I was considering at which of the public-houses I should spend the evening, when suddenly a most terrific thunderstorm came on. The darkness was intense. I thought the Judgment Day had come. I rose up from my seat and ran out of the house in wild despair. After some time I came in again, and fell on my knees (I don't know when I had been on them before); but I could not ask for mercy. I felt that I was doomed, and looked up again and again, expecting to see the world in flames, so certain was I that the end had come and I was not ready. My whole being was convulsed with anguish at the thought of meeting God.

When the storm passed over it seemed as if all the blood in my body had gone, and for several hours I looked like a corpse. At this time I was a strong-nerved young man, knowing no fear, but all my courage failed me when brought face to face with ETERNITY. So will yours, dear reader, if still unsaved. What an awful picture we have of the "Seal day" in Revelation, Chapter 6: "And the kings of the earth, and the great men, and the rich men, and the chief captains, and the mighty men, and every bondman, and every free man, hid themselves in the dens and in the rocks of the mountains; and said to the mountains and rocks, fall on us, and hide us from the face of Him that sitteth on the throne, and from the wrath of the Lamb: for the great day of His wrath is come; and who shall be able to stand?"

I resolved to give up drink and all my sinful ways, and lead, as I thought, a new life.

There was a Methodist Class-Meeting convenient to where I lived, and I asked my wife if she would go with me on the next Sunday to that meeting. She gladly consented to do so, and, I am sure, was delighted to see any change in me.

I cannot describe my feelings the first morning in the Class-Meeting, when the members of the class stood up and told what God had done for them. I could not lift my head; I felt so condemned. I believed there was not a greater wretch on the face of the earth than I. I would have given worlds, had I possessed them, to know my sins forgiven.

I often sat up for several hours through the night, literally trembling from head to foot, thinking I was just about to drop into Hell, but could not utter one word of prayer to God. Sometimes I thought my mind would give way.

Some weeks afterwards I was invited to attend a Methodist "Love-Feast." The minister was a good man, and preached that day with great power. After the sermon a testimony meeting was held, and when this was over a hearty invitation was given to all who were anxious to be saved to come up to what was called the "penitent-form." I immediately responded to the invitation, for I was in great distress of soul, and would have done anything or gone anywhere to find peace. I did not care who saw or laughed at me; my sins, my soul, and Eternity had become such awful realities.

While at the "penitent-form" a very dear servant of Christ endeavoured to show me the way of Salvation. He pointed out to me that all I had to do was to believe the Word of God, and in a little while I persuaded myself to believe that I was saved. (An error which thousands make, and many earnest servants of God make the mistake of dwelling too much on the word *believe* and failing to put Christ and His Work on the cross before the anxious soul.) I then stood up and told the audience that I was converted.

I held to my profession for about three weeks, thinking every day that I was becoming more holy, but I was in great bondage, and could scarcely attend to my work, so afraid was I of sinning.

One day I went to the town, and before I realized where I was, I found myself in a public-house with a full glass of whisky in my hand. I drank it, and immediately felt myself completely under the power of Satan.

I will not describe the awful and shameful scenes which took place that day before the gaze of hundreds of people. I had not hitherto been so publicly exposed. I had truly the experience of Matthew 12:43-45; "the unclean spirit going out of the man, and coming back with seven other spirits more wicked than himself." I felt as though demons were gathered around me, jeering at the man who had so recently professed conversion. I had now brought public disgrace upon myself and my relatives, and thought that God had given me up, and that none of His people would ever speak to me again.

Satan tempted me to destroy myself; I could not rest that night in my house. I deeply pitied my dear wife, because she was joined to such a wretch. Contrary to my expectations, on that very night two godly Methodist class-leaders walked a long way to see me, having heard of the awful day through which I had passed. I shall always remember the kindness of these two servants of God in visiting me under such circumstances.

After this I had seasons of great horror and darkness, and thought God had forsaken me and that His Spirit would never strive with me again. I indulged more freely in drink than I had done in the past, and drank to such excess that on one occasion I found myself away from home, out in a snow-storm, and within a few minutes of a drunkard's hell, had not God in His wondrous grace interposed. It was on a Saturday night—or, rather, early on Sunday morning—and the snow, which was falling heavily, was blown in drifts across the road, in some places several feet deep. My companion assisted me to reach a house, where a light was burning, but the inmates refused to admit us and, as I was quite exhausted, I lay down outside the door. By this time I was sober, and fully aware of my condition. I felt that I was dying fast, and Hell was an awful reality to me at that moment. I vowed if God would deliver me that I would never indulge in intoxicating drink again, and thank God, I never have. Shortly afterwards the door was opened and I was helped into the house, and kindly attended to.

I became unconscious but, after several hours, recovered and was able to walk to my home, which I reached about six o'clock that Sunday morning, where I found my faithful wife waiting for me, hardly expecting again to see me alive. I told her of my resolve never to touch drink again. That was a dismal and depressing Sunday to me. I felt every moment as if the wrath of God were about to descend upon my head.

I went in the evening to my old drunken chum and asked him to go with me to a Gospel meeting which was being held near by. He laughed and said: "We would be nice boys to go to such a place," and I was eventually obliged to go alone.

I cannot describe my feelings as I opened the door

of that meeting-room. As I entered they were
singing, and I felt as though it were Heaven and I as
black as Hell. (Unsaved reader, what will your
feelings be on that day, when all Christless sinners
shall stand exposed in the glare of the Great White
Throne, to be judged by the Son of God, Who shall
sit thereon, surrounded by the angelic hosts and
myriads of the Redeemed; and from that scene to be
banished to the depths of an everlasting Hell, to
weep and gnash the teeth in the Lake which
burneth with fire and brimstone? May God now
open your eyes and lead you to Christ, for His
Name's sake.)

I gave up many of my sinful ways and companions,
and indeed some thought I was a Christian, and
often Satan tried to persuade me that I was: but I
had no peace.

I went on in this way for a short time, until one
night, after rising from my knees, it seemed as if an
audible voice spoke to me and said: "You see you
might as well give up prayer and all hope of being
saved, for you are the man that is born to be
damned. You have tried all means to be saved, and
all have failed." I said: "It is true, I will never pray
again," and I lay down on my bed that night,
resolved to go to Hell.

My anguish of soul was indescribable, as I
thought of how I should have to endure the
unquenchable fire throughout the ceaseless ages of
eternity. As I tossed on my bed, I cried out: "O God,
bid me do anything and I will do it to be saved."
Suddenly the following words flashed across my
mind: "Be ye reconciled to God, for He hath made

Him to be sin for us, Who knew no sin; that we might be made the righteousness of God in Him" 2 Cor. 5:20-21. I felt as though I were standing at the Cross on the day that Christ died, and as I gazed upon His pierced hands and side, the words kept sounding in my ears: "Be ye reconciled to God," and I thought that Jesus looked down upon me and said: "Could I give more for you? I have given My life. Will this not satisfy you?"

This was new to me, as I had thought it was I who had to satisfy God. At once I felt my heart going out in thankfulness to the Lord Jesus Who had died to save me, and as I thanked Him joy unspeakable filled my soul, and I said to my wife: "I am saved." All my fears of Hell vanished. I could truly say in the language of the poet:—

"Soon as my all I ventured on the atoning
    blood,
The Holy Spirit entered, and I was born of
    God."

Chapter 2
1869-1876
FIRST PUBLIC SERVICE

My desire now was to tell to others what the Lord had done for me. I first went to those against whom I had had any bitter feelings, and told them that I was saved, and that I had forgiven everyone. I felt as though I could have taken all the world in my arms to Christ.

My next step was to gather my companions into a school-room early on Sunday mornings and read the Scriptures and pray with them. On the first Sunday about sixteen came. They continued coming every Lord's Day, and seemed interested. The first sign of blessing was when one of them, a young man named George Davidson, came to my house to tell me he had been saved on the previous night. He also told me his cousin had been walking about most of the night, unable to sleep for anxiety about his soul, and sought my advice as to what could be done for him.

I had not at this time thought of preaching, but I asked him to bring his cousin and some others with him on the following Wednesday night, and I would endeavour to speak to them of Christ. Seven came. I gave out the hymn:—

"I hear the words of love,
I gaze upon the blood,
I see the mighty sacrifice,
And I have peace with God."

I cannot describe the feeling that came over us while the hymn was being sung. Some turned quite pale, and three or four of the seven professed conversion. I was so filled with the Spirit of God, Who had enabled me to speak with such liberty, that I was convinced that He had called me to preach the Gospel to the world.

I arranged a meeting for the next Saturday night, and gave a general invitation to all the people around the district to attend. My joy and love for souls was so great that I could scarcely take my food. The news soon spread, and on the night of the meeting the school-room was filled long before the time announced. We commenced by singing —

"Rock of ages, cleft for me,
Let me hide myself in Thee:
Let the water and the blood,
From Thy riven side which flowed,
Be of sin the double cure:
Save me from its guilt and power."

I then prayed and read a portion of Luke 13: "Except ye repent ye shall all likewise perish." Amid the cries of the anxious and the shouts of new-born souls, I continued speaking for about three and a half hours.

The scene was indescribable: fathers, mothers, and children crying together for mercy—some of them hardened blasphemers. The meeting did not break up until after midnight, and most of the audience returned at six o'clock the same morning, and we continued almost all that day.

I sent word to the places where I thought I had committed the most sin, that I was going to tell them of Jesus, but we could get no halls large enough to hold the people who came.

In most of these places we had not long commenced our meeting until we could hear the cries of the anxious from several parts of the building.

An Orange Lodge hall was situated next door to where I lived, and so many of its members professed conversion that within a few weeks they broke up their drums and made covers for hymn-books with the heads of them.

The Methodists throughout the district invited me to hold meetings in their preaching-houses, and the Lord blessed us mightily. The first Twelfth of July we had a fellowship-meeting, and nearly two hundred of a band marched through the country singing praises to God.

I went on for several years, working with my hands and preaching almost every week-night, and three or four times on Sunday. The interest so increased that at last I had scarcely time to attend to my employment, and had often to work all night to get time for the meetings.

I had now a longing desire to enter upon new ground, but was so situated that I could not go very far from home.

About this time a Mr. Barton, of Dundalk, who had heard of me, wrote saying that he and a few others were thinking of establishing an unsectarian Society for the preaching of the Gospel. I looked upon this as God's way of bringing me forth.

I met Mr. Barton, and we conducted a meeting together at Coalisland. The Society was not formed for some months afterwards.

ARMAGH, 1875

I held a number of meetings in the town of Armagh. On one occasion I went into Irish Street (entirely a Roman Catholic district), and, when I gave out a hymn, the inhabitants gathered round me in hundreds. I thought I was going to have a large meeting, but soon a man in the crowd shouted out: "Begone." I replied that I had no intention of going until I had preached the Gospel. Immediately four men caught hold of me, and I could hear them shouting from all quarters: "Kill him." A large dog was brought and held to my throat, but God shut his mouth, and he did not attempt to injure me. After some time I was rescued by the police, who guarded me to the market-house, where I had previously arranged to preach the same evening.

I returned to the town on the following Tuesday, which was a market-day, and took my stand in the open air. Opposition was again shown towards me, but the Lord over-ruled it, and I was enabled to preach there almost every market-day for a year; although I was frequently roughly treated and often covered with mud.

On St. Patrick's Day, a Christian man came to help me to sing, but they chased him down the street and beat him severely. However, they did not interfere with me, and I preached to a large audience, mostly Roman Catholic, for almost an hour.

Some time afterwards, while visiting a watering-place about twenty miles from this town, a woman told me that she had been saved while I was preaching in Armagh, through the words: "He was wounded for our transgressions, He was bruised for our iniquities, the chastisement of our peace was upon Him, and with His stripes we are healed" Isaiah 53:5.

DUNDALK, 1875

Mr. Barton asked me to go to Dundalk for a short time. I went, visited around that district, and had some blessing, especially at a place called Hawthorn Hill, where the Lord saved a number of souls.

In a place named Jonesboro', which is about six miles from Dundalk, I preached for about an hour in the open air, as I had been unable to secure a hall. The people in the locality were mostly Roman Catholic, and when I had finished I was surrounded by a hostile crowd who completely hedged me in. An aged priest was amongst them. I asked them if I had said anything to offend. "Not one word," said the priest, "You are quite right to preach the Gospel. Come back and preach whenever you please." I thanked him, and thanked God for His deliverance.

I was greatly helped by Mr. Barton. He established me in the Word of God, and I esteemed him very highly. He has been greatly used of God in the spreading of the Gospel. I remarked to him one day that I should not stay much longer in Dundalk, as I was anxious to carry the Gospel into other places. He then told me of a village called Darkley, in the County Armagh, where a meeting had been held every week for almost ten years, but very little blessing had been manifested; so I arranged with him to take up the work there as soon as convenient.

DARKLEY, 1875-1876

I held my first meeting here on a Sunday night. The hall was empty when I entered, but before long my audience began to arrive. They did not, however, recognise me as the preacher.

I sat for some time, while they laughed and jested, and shouted out: "The preacher is not coming tonight." I believe God wished me to see the class of people to whom I had to preach. When I ascended the platform a wonderful change took place. Every head was bowed in shame, and none could look up.

I took for my subject Jonah 1 verse 6, "What meanest thou, O sleeper? arise, call upon thy God, if so be that God will think upon us, that we perish not."

I was much helped of the Lord in warning the sinner to "flee from the wrath to come." A deep solemnity pervaded the meeting, and one young woman was brought to Christ that night. A remarkable work of God commenced, and in a few nights the cries of the anxious were heard above the singing, and soon the place was too small to hold the people.

I received a message from the Roman Catholics,

of whom there were several hundred in that place,
requesting me to preach outside, before going into
the hall, as they desired to hear, but dared not go in.
This I gladly consented to do, and about three
hundred listened with rapt attention every night,
until the priest came to know of it, and ordered
every door to be closed. Yet they sent me word to
continue to preach, as they could hear me inside
their houses. I had a good voice, thank God, and
went on preaching, though I did not see one of my
audience.

On one occasion, just as I had commenced
speaking, a Roman Catholic boy, who was lying
very ill, on hearing me, asked his mother the cause
of the noise. She replied, "It's the preacher." He
requested her to lift him up to the window, and he
died ere I had concluded. I trust that he accepted
Christ as his Saviour, and, through the Precious
Blood, passed to be forever with the Lord.

Nine of one family were brought to Christ here
during this mission.

The blessing spread throughout the country for
miles around, and it was not unusual to hear hymns
of praise to God being sung at midnight in the open
air.

A brother named John Bothwell, a native of this
place, and his wife helped me all through the work.
He became a real shepherd to the young converts.
We endeavoured, as far as we were able, to establish
them in the Word of God, and commenced a Sunday
morning meeting at an early hour for that purpose.
This was a great benefit to the babes in Christ, and
many unconverted were brought to know the Lord

in these gatherings. On one occasion I had to walk all night in order to attend this meeting. I became very hungry and sleepy, and had to rest twice by the way.

After the work had gone on for a short time, Mr. Bothwell and some others began to be very dissatisfied with the state of things in the denominations to which they belonged. They thought the best thing they could do was to search the Scriptures and compare the primitive assemblies with the modern Churches. This they did earnestly for some weeks, and came to the conclusion that there was little comparison or likeness, as the early Christians met together on the first day of the week to remember the Lord in the breaking of bread, without any man to preside, or any head or lordship but Christ, and were addressed by the names of brethren, Christians, or saints.

Although at this time they had never met or heard of those whom the people called Plymouth Brethren, yet they arranged to meet in Mr. Bothwell's house on the first day of the week to remember the Lord in the breaking of bread, in accordance with 1 Corinthians 11:23-25, and Acts 20:7.

They continued to assemble thus, amid the scoffs and reproaches of many in the neighbourhood. A short time afterwards Mr. William McLean, of Peterhead, paid them a visit, and taught them believers' baptism by immersion, as contained in the Scriptures (see Acts 8:36-38: "And as they went on their way they came unto a certain water; and the eunuch said: 'See here is water; what doth hinder me to be baptized?' And Philip said: 'If thou believest with all thine heart, thou mayest.' And he answered and said: 'I believe that Jesus Christ is the Son of God.' And he commanded the chariot to stand still; and they went both down into the water, both Philip and the eunuch, and he baptized him.")

On one occasion Mr. McLean baptized ten in a river in this vicinity. It was a St. Patrick's Day, 17th of March, and the people working in the fields thought at first that they were going to "drown the shamrock," but when they saw them going into the water they shouted out that someone was being drowned, and came in crowds to see what was the matter. The baptism was over before they reached the place, but brother McLean was obliged to hasten away, as they blamed him for being the cause of what they characterized as unseemly conduct.

He returned later, and baptized ten others, but had to flee again, as the father of one of the Christians whom he had baptized came, armed with a spade, declaring that he would kill him.

Notwithstanding all the opposition and ridicule, the Lord continued to bless, and soon the little assembly numbered almost one hundred; and many have been raised up amongst them to preach the Gospel and to minister to the saints.

I often tried to preach on the streets of Keady (which is a short distance from Darkley) on market and fair days, but on every occasion I was so violently treated by the opponents of the Gospel that I had eventually to desist from any further effort to preach in the open air in this town.

BESSBROOK (FIRST VISIT), 1876

This was another place of much blessing. I had been invited to preach in a certain meeting-house there, but was afterwards informed that the Committee, on reconsidering the matter, had decided not to proceed with the mission, and I was advised not to come. I replied that I was determined to go, and that I could preach in the open air.

On coming into Newry, on my way to Bessbrook, I was told of a gentleman named Egan, a true Christian, who would be glad to accompany me. I called upon him, and he and another young man came with me. When we arrived at Bessbrook, we marched through the streets singing. The inhabitants seemed impressed, and listened very attentively while we conducted a most solemn meeting in the centre of the town.

One young woman, belonging to the Society of Friends, stood at a distance, as she afterwards said, ashamed to come near. Yet God spoke to her where she stood, and she was led to Christ. She became an active Christian worker, and all evangelists visiting here were heartily welcomed at her mother's house.

The Friends (known as "The Quakers") proposed lending us their Tabernacle in which to conduct our services, but the attendance was so large that we were obliged to continue the meetings in a field close by, and frequently saw almost one thousand people remain at these until ten o'clock at night.

On one occasion I was interrupted while speaking by four persons shouting out that they had just been saved.

The Spirit of God moved on the hearts of the people throughout the whole country for miles around, but some religious leaders raised active opposition. One Presbyterian minister, however, who was a true friend and a lover of the Gospel, stated publicly in our meeting (touching with his finger the white tie which he wore) that this was a mere Roman emblem, and that he made no distinction between clergymen and lay preachers.

He had previously been invited to conduct a service in a church in this district but, after he had made such a statement, the arrangement was cancelled.

In one of our most solemn gatherings, when I announced the after-meeting, the entire congregation remained. We did not know, however, that the Devil had about eighty men, ready to create a disturbance. As soon as I had made the announcement the ringleader came forward, in a menacing manner, evidently with the intention of assaulting me. Some of my friends withstood him, and in a short time there was fearful panic, and blood was flowing freely. The police were sent for, and obtained the names of my assailants, against whom summonses were afterwards issued. All, however, was for the furtherance of the Gospel.

Mr. Richardson, of Moyallen, kindly invited the young converts to tea at his house, and between eighty and ninety responded to the invitation.

I was requested by Mr. M'Clelland, of Slatemills, to come and preach in his store. I did so, and the power of God was mightily manifested, and many were led to Christ.

Chapter 3

MAGHERAFELT, COUNTY DERRY, 1876

After leaving Bessbrook I went to Magherafelt, where I commenced in an old Courthouse. I continued for several nights and, having perceived no visible signs of blessing, I remarked to the brother with whom I lodged that I thought it strange that there was so little interest in the meetings. He replied that he had never seen much interest evinced in any religious movement in that town. I was very anxious, however, to see the hand of God in the awakening and salvation of souls.

One night, after our meeting, I was having tea at a friend's house when I received a message that someone wished to speak to me at the door. It was a young man, trembling from head to foot, who said that he could not go to bed without knowing his sins forgiven. I went out on to the street with him and, while I was pointing him to the Saviour, he passed from death unto life.

At the same time a woman had called at my lodgings, enquiring for me, as she was in great anxiety about her soul. This encouraged me, and on the following nights we had many more such anxious enquirers.

I asked all who were really anxious, and who would like to be spoken to personally, to attend a meeting on the following Saturday night. About sixty came, and we had a most solemn time.

25

TUBBERMORE, 1876

Mr. Carson, a Baptist minister, of Tubbermore, invited me to hold a series of services in his chapel. I went, and we had a most remarkable time of blessing.

On the first night the house was nearly full, and the power of God was so manifest that both saved and unsaved were in tears. Five of Mr. Carson's children and his servant were under conviction. It was a most affecting sight, and one which I shall not soon forget, when his eldest son professed conversion. His father threw his arms around him, and shouted out with joy before all the meeting, "My son, my son." The people wept aloud.

In a few nights the meeting-house was not large enough to hold the numbers who came, many having to stand outside. Almost one thousand attended nightly, and the meetings frequently continued for about six hours. Often people were to be seen coming in from the country several hours before the appointed time of our meeting, so anxious were they to secure a seat.

I do not know exactly how many professed conversion, but Mr. Carson baptised ninety-six who were converted during this mission.

My soul was often grieved to see the inhabitants of large districts living in spiritual darkness, with no one to tell them the Gospel in its simplicity. At this time I visited all the fairs and markets held in the towns and villages around, generally preaching from a farmer's cart. It was a new thing to many.

MONEYMORE, 1876

We had a platform erected on Moneymore Fair Hill, from which I preached. On one occasion a man turned away in a great rage and, referring to me, he said, "He is the Devil"; but while we were singing that beautiful hymn—

"There were ninety and nine that safely lay
    In the shelter of the fold,
But one was out on the hills away,
    Far off from the gates of gold,
Away on the mountains, wild and bare,
    Away from the tender shepherd's care."

he was drawn back to the meeting, convicted of sin, and brought to Christ. He afterwards became a great friend of mine.

A Mr. Denning united with me for a month for the fairs, markets, and open-air work. He was very active for the Lord, and fearless of men. We preached twice a day, not without a great deal of opposition, as we sometimes went to Roman Catholic districts.

MAGHERA, 1876

We commenced in Maghera on a market-day, marching through the streets singing. The marketing was almost entirely given up, and a large crowd, mostly Roman Catholic, assembled in the market square, where we preached for a long time. Many of our audience were in tears, while others mocked and raged.

We announced a meeting to be held in the same place on the following market-day, which was a week hence.

We were lodging some distance outside Maghera, and on the day appointed for our meeting, as we drew near to the town, we were accosted by two magistrates and an Inspector of police, who informed us that if we were seen in the town we should be torn to pieces. They took us to an hotel and locked us in, but Mr. Denning demanded that we should get free. They thereupon unlocked the door, but said that they had not a sufficient force to protect us from violence, should we persist in our determination to preach in the market-square. We replied that we would accept the responsibility.

By this time a large crowd had gathered outside the hotel, and as we came out every eye was upon us. We succeeded, with difficulty, in making our way through the people, and reached the centre of the town unmolested, where we took our stand on the steps of the Methodist Chapel. The people thronged around, and we sang a hymn. Mr. Denning whispered to me to speak where I stood. I did so, and they listened very attentively.

We then invited them into the chapel, and in a few minutes it was packed to over-flowing, many Roman Catholics being amongst them. Mr. Denning and I both addressed the audience, after which we went down and spoke to them personally about their souls. We left the town the same evening, no violence whatever having been shown towards us.

DRAPERSTOWN, 1876

I had preached alone several times before in this town and, although I had met with a great deal of opposition, I had frequently seen many in tears while the Word was being declared. Some friends endeavoured to dissuade us from going, stating that if we did so we should be violently treated. The Lord gave us courage, however, and we went.

We had what I believe was a marvellous deliverance one night on our way from this place. We had been preaching in the market-house, where they had tried to suffocate us with cayenne pepper, the audience having been obliged to run out almost choked. A window had been broken with stones, and drums were beaten at the door while our service was being held.

After the meeting several friends entreated us not to go to our home (which was seven miles distant) by the direct road, as a plot had been laid to take our lives; but we trusted God for protection and went.

The night was pitch dark, and when about two miles out of the town we saw a number of men by the roadside. The driver was about to stop the car, but I told him to drive on, and a few seconds later the road behind us was lighted up by a huge flame, but we were safe.

On another occasion Mr. Denning and I received several messages that if we preached in the town we should be roughly handled. Still we felt convinced that we should go, and looked to the Lord to preserve us from injury.

We took our stand, at the time appointed, in the market-square, and in a short time a large crowd of people had formed a circle around us. While I was speaking a fierce-looking man, apparently the ring-leader, stepped forward. I walked towards him and preached right into his face. He stood for a moment trembling, and then went back to the crowd without saying a word, but in a few moments he again came forward. I met him in the same way, looked him straight in the face, and went on preaching. He appeared confounded, remained for a few seconds, and again returned to his companions. I was not interrupted further. There was complete silence, except for the sound of sobbing. Many were in tears. The power of God was very evident, and the results of that meeting will only be fully manifested when the Lord comes.

We preached at night in a schoolroom on the Lough Shore, and visited throughout the country during the day. One day in our visiting we found ourselves in a Roman Catholic district. In one house which we visited Mr. Denning spoke to a woman who was smoking a pipe. All the time he was talking to her she kept puffing the smoke into his face. On leaving this house we separated, he going in one direction and I in another.

In the next house I visited there was a hardened-looking old woman, engaged in domestic duties. As usual, without any preliminaries, I immediately told her that my business was to point sinners to the "Lamb of God which taketh away the sin of the world." She turned to me and said, "Do you see that door?" I replied that I did. "Well," she continued, "if you mention anything in this house, except about the Holy Mother of God, St. Peter, and Jesus, out you go." I said I would not speak of anyone else; indeed I thought she had given me a very big subject. I spoke for a long time from the Word of God, and when I had finished the house was almost filled with a very rough class of people. One big masculine-looking girl shouted out that I should be burned, so I thought it time to take my departure, and when I came out they all followed me. I then saw Mr. Denning coming towards me with a mob after him. The two parties joined and came after us for a long way, stoning us all the time. I have never seen anyone take such treatment better than Mr. Denning, as amidst it all he kept smiling.

We ventured into another house, but they immediately turned us out. In the next house we entered a dear man and his wife broke down while we were speaking to them and cried for mercy. We trust they found it.

BELLAGHY, DECEMBER, 1876

I had been told that this was a very wicked town, and that three of the Lord's servants, very godly men, had travelled a long way to preach the Gospel there. One Sunday afternoon they had held a meeting in the Orange Hall, but had met with such vigorous opposition from the local religious leaders, and had suffered such violence at the hands of the people, that they decided not to hold any further services in the town.

When I heard this I thought it would be the very

place for me, and shortly afterwards I went there.

When I came near the town I asked the driver, who was a Roman Catholic, to stop the car, as I wished to spend a short time in prayer. He appeared greatly startled at this request, but, nevertheless, did as I desired. After prayer we drove on, and I took my stand in the main street.

The night was very dark, and the streets were badly lighted, but about one hundred people gathered around me. I told them I had come to preach the Gospel, that I intended doing so every night for some time, if the weather permitted, and asked if there was any person in the crowd who would supply me with a chair upon which to stand. Someone sarcastically replied that I could have a broken one. I said that would do all right.

On the following night I enquired from a shopkeeper near at hand if he had an old box which I could purchase. He told me there was one in his yard, and that I might take it free of charge.

I secured the box and took my stand on the other side of the street, opposite his shop. The audience that evening was much larger than on the previous night, but they quickly scattered when stones, pots, kettles, and cans began to be hurled amongst them. Some were hurt, and the noise was awful. I told them that I would not leave until I was knocked down, and that, if the Lord permitted me, I should be back again on the following night.

When I returned the next evening I was surprised to find the shop opposite to where I had been preaching closed, and four policemen standing by. When I mounted my platform—the old box—the sergeant came forward and told me that I should not be allowed to preach there, as the merchants had been obliged to close their shops through fear of a disturbance. I asked him where I could speak, and he replied that he could not tell.

I lifted my box, crossed the street, and took my stand opposite a public-house door. The police followed me, and said this was worse than the other stand. I said I had come to preach the Gospel, and that I must preach here tonight. While the police and I were contending a crowd (mostly of able-bodied men) had gathered. They ordered the police to leave me alone, and shouted to me to get on to the box and preach. I did so, and held my meeting without further interruption, and the power of God was mightily manifested that night.

A solemn awe pervaded every meeting afterwards, and the numbers increased nightly until my audience was about seven hundred. I continued here for eleven successive nights, and many were convicted of sin and brought to Christ. I then commenced meetings in a house, and the Lord blessed wonderfully.

At this time I was under the auspices of the Irish Evangelization Society, whose Hon. Secretary was Mr. Barton. He received many slanderous communications respecting me from some of the religious leaders of Bellaghy, who vigorously opposed my work there. But the Lord in this also over-ruled all things to His glory, so that these opponents of the Gospel were utterly confounded. How very solemn it is to attempt to hinder the work of God!

I visited another place in this neighbourhood and, as usual, took my stand in the open air. I had not long been speaking when a woman came out of a house convenient and invited me inside to hold a meeting. I did so, although the house had a most wretched appearance, and my audience (which immediately followed me) was a miserably poor and illiterate class of people.

While I was preaching a dog was thrown in through the window, but this did not deter me. I continued as though no interruption had taken place, and announced a meeting for the following night.

The next day this poor woman's son had been so severely beaten by the enemies of the Gospel in the locality for permitting me to preach in her house that when I returned I found the door was closed against me. But as I had come to preach, I took up my position on the street. Some opposition, however, was shown, and she again invited me to her house. I went, but found it impossible to hold another meeting there. On my way home we were followed for a long distance by a mob, and when they were about to close in upon us I told the driver to stop the car. I then got off to meet them but, strange to say, they all fled.

Chapter 4

CASTLEBELLINGHAM, 1877

About this time a Castlebellingham lady wrote to the Society, requesting them to send an Evangelist down there to hold a few meetings. Mr. Barton asked me to go, and I consented.

When I reached the lady's house, and informed her that I was the preacher, she seemed somewhat disappointed in my appearance, as I was more like a ploughman than an evangelist, having walked a long distance on a very muddy road.

She enquired of me how long I had been engaged in this work. I told her I had been preaching the Gospel for a few years. I waited while she went to get a conveyance to take me to the village. She soon returned with a machine, I was placed in the seat beside the driver, and quickly conveyed to lodgings suitable to my appearance.

Our first meeting was attended by a fair number of very respectable people. I took for my subject Isaiah 5:14, "Therefore hell hath enlarged herself and opened her mouth without measure, and their glory, and their multitude, and their pomp, and he that rejoiceth, shall descend into it." I felt the presence and power of God in the meeting, and we all seemed to realise that the Lord was with us.

The lady's demeanour towards me greatly changed, and afterwards, when writing to Mr. Barton, she stated that she never thought there was such a verse in the Scriptures as the one which I had quoted and which I had taken for my subject.

At the close of my first meeting a gentleman invited me to his house to be the guest of himself and his family, whose invitation I gladly accepted.

The Lord spoke to many souls during this mission, and the Coming Day will declare results.

On the morning I left the village I felt strongly impressed to go through a large demesne on my way to the station. When going through I saw a little cottage, at which I resolved to call. A man, his wife and children lived in it; the man looked very sickly, and told me he had been discharged from the Army owing to bad health. I commenced speaking to him about his soul and the necessity of being born again, at which both he and his wife got into a fearful rage. Still I went on and delivered my message, and knelt down and prayed that God would save them.

About a year afterwards I received a communication from this man, requesting me to visit him, if possible, as he had never had peace of mind since the time I had called at his cottage.

I was in County Derry at the time, and so could not comply with his urgent request.

Three weeks later I was at a Believers' Meeting in Dundalk. The lady whom I first went to see at Castlebellingham was also there. She said she had a message for me from the man in the demesne (who had now gone to be with the Lord), who had told her, if she should see me, to let me know he had been led to Christ through the words I had spoken to him in the cottage on the day I left. I did praise the Lord.

DUNLEER, 1877

I spent so much time at the cottage in the demesne at Castlebellingham that I missed the train and had to walk five miles up the line to Dunleer. I spoke to some of the navvies on the way, and one man told me he had never heard of a Bible in his life.

I visited almost all the Protestant families in the village, but was unable to secure a house in which to hold a meeting. I then visited the country around and entered a house in which was a young woman. I told her I had come sixty miles with a message from God for her. She immediately fell down on the floor and screamed aloud. I felt a little upset, but continued speaking and praying with her. She found peace through trusting in Christ.

I left the house and after walking a short distance I met a man. I asked him if he knew where I could have a room in which to preach the Gospel. He proposed to let me have his house, and we arranged a meeting. To my surprise I found it was the home of the young woman who had professed conversion, and that the man whom I had met was her father. How blessed it is to be led by the Lord alone!

WARRENPOINT, 1877

I held a series of meetings on the Strand here for about three weeks. Sometimes the opposition was very great, a mob doing their utmost to prevent my being heard. Still the Lord gave the Word in power.

I lodged in the house of a family of Roman Catholics, but they insisted on my leaving. I had, however, the privilege of praying and speaking with them.

BALLYCASTLE, 1877

This was the next town which I visited. An annual fair was held here, which lasted for almost a week. A lady in the district wrote to the Society, asking them to send an Evangelist down to preach. It was arranged that I should go, and I arrived at her house on the day previous to the commencement of the fair.

On the following morning I invited her to come with me and help me to sing. She seemed surprised at this request, and told her sister what I desired. "Certainly go, and I will go with you," her sister replied, and they both accompanied me.

The streets were very muddy, as there had been heavy rain on the previous day. We took our stand together and commenced to sing a hymn, but had not got quite through it when we were badly smeared with mud, which was freely hurled at us. I preached for an hour and, before I had finished speaking, my face was completely covered. The ladies stood nobly by me all the time, and when the meeting was over distributed tracts to the by-standers.

BALLINTOY, 1877

I went to Ballintoy, where a fair was being held, and preached in the open air. A circus was in town, but they stopped their performance while I spoke.

That night I stayed with the circus performers in a lodging-house. I read and talked with them until 1 a.m.

There were thirteen of us in the small dwelling. Some lay on benches, but I had the best bed in the house, and they were very kind to me. When I asked the old landlady in the morning the amount of my bill, she replied, "Tuppence, dear."

BALLYMENA (FIRST VISIT), 1877

I came to this town on the invitation of the Baptist Pastor, and commenced meetings in his chapel. On the first night the attendance was very small. The minister told me it was difficult to get the people to come in, so I felt led to go out and compel them, and on the second night I and a few others took our stand at a street corner about an hour previous to the time specified for the meeting to commence.

We had not been long there when a policeman came forward and enquired of me if I were a stranger in the town. I replied that I was. "I thought so," said he, "or you would not be preaching here." I stated that it was my custom to preach in the open air, to which he replied, "You can't preach here, you are obstructing the thoroughfare." I pointed out to him that the thoroughfare was quite clear, and he told me that if I proceeded further I should have to go to the barracks with him, as I was gathering a crowd. I said that was what I had come there to do. We sang a hymn, I preached the Gospel, and we then sang down to the meeting-house, a large crowd following us in.

We again resorted to the open air on the next evening, and as we were about to commence four policemen appeared on the scene. One of them warned me that if I were not off the street in five minutes I should be taken to the barracks.

I replied that, if it pleased them, they might do so, but that I did not intend to leave until I had preached the Gospel. He took my name and address, and when I was at dinner on the following day two policemen came to me and handed me two summonses. I said to them that they should have brought me another one, as I intended preaching in the same place on that night. The next day they again appeared and handed me a third summons. "Go on with the summonses," said I to them, "and I will go on with the preaching."

By this time the attendance at our open-air meetings was so great that the passers-by could scarcely get through the crowd, and our large meeting-house was packed to overflowing.

The Spirit of God wrought in the hearts of the people, and many were convicted of sin. On one occasion a Roman Catholic man held the chair on which I stood while I was speaking.

When the time for appearing to answer the summonses arrived, the Courthouse was packed, and when my name was called most of those present rose to their feet. The charge having been read out, the presiding magistrate asked me if I had anything to say. I replied: "If I am free I am going to preach in the same place tonight." "And we give you full liberty to preach and sing wherever you please throughout the town," said he, "and the police, instead of interfering with you, must protect you."

The scene that night was indescribable. Hundreds stood around us at our meeting in the street, and for several weeks we continued there with great blessing. Since then the streets of Ballymena have been open for the preaching of the Gospel. "All praise to Him Who sits upon the Throne."

ADDRESS (COUNTY TYRONE), 1877

Mr. Ashe, the Rector of the Irish Church, invited me to commence meetings in the schoolroom here. I did so, and soon the attendance was so large that the room would not hold the people. We thought it better to have our meetings in the church, which was much larger, but soon it also was filled to overflowing. We continued the meetings for several weeks, and many precious souls were brought "from darkness to light."

At the request of Mr. Ashe, I conducted a funeral service in the church. This was a new experience for me, and it was also a new thing for the people to see anyone other than a clergyman take such a service. After the coffin had been removed, and almost all had gone, I saw a woman weeping bitterly. I enquired of her if the departed one were a relation. "No," she replied, "but I am in distress about my soul." And while they were burying the dead I had the joy of seeing this anxious woman pass from death unto life.

I stayed with Mr. Ashe, and have the happiest recollections of both him and his family. His love for

souls was great. When visiting around the neighbourhood he rarely allowed anyone to pass without
putting the question: "Do you know your sins
forgiven?"

About sixty or seventy people assembled at the
Rectory every morning, and I preached to them the
Gospel.

At this time there had been a prolonged
discussion going on amongst the leaders of the Irish
Church respecting the revision of the Prayer Book.
The question of baptismal regeneration, which sets
forth that a child by its baptism is made a member of
Christ, a child of God, and an inheritor of eternal
life, had been under review. Mr. Ashe was one of
those who spoke in very pronounced language
against the retention of this in the book, and
strongly advocated the Scriptural teaching that
"except a man be born again he cannot see the
Kingdom of God." He held that only those who
knew their sins forgiven were qualified to partake
of the Lord's Supper, and was opposed to the
prevalent idea that baptism and confirmation effect
a spiritual change upon the subjects of these
ordinances.

The Word of God teaches that it is only believers
who should be baptised ("then they that gladly
received the Word were baptised." Acts 2:41), and
that only believers should partake of the Lord's
Supper. ("And they continued steadfastly in the
Apostles' doctrine and fellowship and in breaking of
bread, and in prayers." Acts 2:42.)

The Apostle Paul points out that this is done on
the first day of the week: "And upon the first day of

the week, when the disciples came together to break bread" (Acts 20:7). This at once suggests to us that it was on the first day of every week that they came together, just in the same sense as the Jews understood that they were to "remember the Sabbath Day to keep it holy."

The sure and certain hope of a glorious resurrection is only for those who fall asleep in Christ (1 Thessalonians 4:14). Note the words *in Christ.*

DONEGAL, 1877

Mrs. Graham, a very active Christian worker, wrote to Mr. Barton, asking if I were free to come and hold a series of meetings in a new hall which had just been built in that town. I decided to go. An American evangelist named Leonard had conducted Gospel meetings in the place about a year previous, and the Lord had blessed his labours.

Mrs. Graham had interested herself in the continuation of the work but, as many of the religious leaders opposed her and used their influence in preventing her from obtaining a house where the Gospel could be preached, she had been obliged to set about having a hall built.

Several friends subscribed liberally to this object and to the amazement of some, and the amusement of others, at the idea of building such a large hall in a place so comparatively small, and in the face of such strong opposition, the building was completed, and was now ready for meetings to be commenced.

The presence and power of God were manifested in my first meeting, and in a few nights the audience was so great that the hall was not large enough to hold the people. I continued here for three weeks, and many came from a distance to the meetings, some even travelling fourteen miles; and souls were saved every night.

KILLETRE, 1877

I responded to the invitation of the Rector of the Episcopal Church to conduct a few meetings at this place. He was, in some ways, a peculiar man, but had a heart for the work of God. He had so advertised the meetings that about five hundred were present on the first night.

He had a grand choir, which he informed me was the best in Ireland. It consisted of twelve young women and his son, who was the leader. After the first night, however, I dispensed with the choir.

The Lord manifested His presence in our first meeting, and many were broken down.

On the second night we continued until a late hour and, as many were anxious to remain even later, it was with difficulty we dispersed the gathering.

We held a meeting in the Rector's dining-room every morning at eleven o'clock. Almost one hundred attended regularly, and many were brought to Christ at these meetings.

ARDARA, 1877

From Killetre I went to Ardara, where I preached in a Methodist Chapel, and on the second night about twenty professed to be saved.

DOORAN, 1877

A few earnest Christians requested me to go to this mountainous district, stating that they had asked Mr. Leonard to go, but he had been prevented by some religious opponents of the Gospel. They asserted that if I went and preached there, as I had done in Donegal, I should see a repetition of the "Revival of 1859."

I replied that, God willing, I would go, no matter what opposition I had to encounter.

Accompanied by the Methodist minister of Ardara, I went to Dooran. We had a long drive over the mountains in a terrific storm. Our horse was a most stubborn animal, frequently stopping on the way, and it was with difficulty that we got it to move on. We had to get off the car several times and walk, and everything seemed against our reaching our destination.

When we arrived the meeting-house was filled with people, notwithstanding the severe storm. Immediately I entered I felt the presence of the Lord, and when I commenced to preach an indescribable power fell upon the whole congregation, and cries for mercy were heard from people in many parts of the building.

Afterwards in some of these meetings I had occasionally to stop speaking, as some would stand up and shout: "Glory to God," while others fell prostrate on the floor in anguish of soul, and cried aloud for mercy.

Eventually I had to stop preaching altogether, and had just to look on and see the Lord working.

Sometimes there would be almost one hundred in one place crying for mercy; in another quarter a number were congregated praying for them, whilst others went amongst them pointing them to Christ. Again, a dozen or so would be standing, after finding peace, praising God aloud.

I have frequently heard in these meetings three different hymns sung at the same time. Some might say: "What confusion!" Yet each appeared to be in the presence of God and praising Him with a full heart and in the language of such hymns as demonstrated their individual blessings.

A solemn incident occurred at this time which had a striking and far-reaching effect. It spoke loudly to us in those days, and should yet help us ever to bear in mind the words spoken by our Lord Himself to His disciples, when rebuking them for their action in forbidding others to do service for God because they did not follow them. (See Mark 9:38 to 40.) A clergyman denounced the work from the pulpit, and characterised it as being the work of the Devil. A short time afterwards, when we had just returned home from the meeting, we heard two loud peals of thunder, and in the morning we were astonished to learn that the church of this clergyman had been struck by lightning and shattered to pieces.

We went to see it, and it presented an awful spectacle. The fire had been hurled a distance of one hundred yards from the building. Seats, walls, windows, and the great organ were one mass of ruins. The thoroughfares leading to the church were crowded with people going to see the strange sight, while they solemnly discussed the remarkable language of the minister regarding us which he had uttered a few days previously.

We had a wonderful time that night. I literally trembled in the meeting. God seemed to be present in awful majesty. I announced a meeting for the next Lord's Day to commence at nine o'clock in the morning. Long before that hour the roads were thronged with people on their way to attend it. Their church had been destroyed and no other place had been arranged for service that day. We continued the meeting until about one o'clock, and almost thirty professed conversion. That was my last meeting in this place. The parting scene is indescribable. It seemed as if Heaven had already begun: every face was wet with tears, parents kissed their children, friends greeted each other, and my hand was crushed and pained with shaking hands in bidding "Good-bye."

I had arranged to preach in the town of Donegal, which was eight miles distant, at four and eight o'clock, that same evening. Many of the people walked all the way from Dooran to these meetings.

I had the privilege of sleeping in the room in which dear Gideon Ouseley slept.

Chapter 5

LAST WORK IN CONNECTION WITH THE IRISH EVANGELIZATION SOCIETY, 1877

I had often been exercised about leaving the Irish Evangelization Society. I had learned from the Word of God truths which I believed I should teach and practise, and which the conditions of the Society debarred me from carrying into effect.

I was very much troubled as to what step I should take, but just about this time and shortly before I left Donegal, three young men, who had been recently converted, asked me if I would baptize them. I was much surprised to see how these young men, away in that dark district, with no man to teach them, had so soon learned from the Scriptures the truth of Believers' Baptism, whilst many others in more enlightened places failed to grasp this plain command and very important Christian ordinance. I felt condemned to have to tell them that I would not. They asked me if I myself were baptized. I replied that I was. "Why, then, will you not baptize us?" they enquired. I told them it was against the rules. "What rules?" they asked. "The rules of the Society," I said.

I can assure you I felt humbled in the presence of those simple-minded Scripturally-taught young men of Donegal. I came home with a sad heart, and for a whole week I cried to God for grace and guidance, so that I might act for Himself. I had a wife and five children to provide for; still I could not think of going on where I could not practise and teach all of my Lord's commandments. I asked my wife if she was willing to break stones with me, and she replied that she was.

I then sat down and wrote my resignation, which I sent to Mr. Barton. He requested me to meet him on the following day, and I did so. He was very much surprised at my decision, but I told him plainly that I could not withstand the words of the Lord Jesus and His command: "Go ye, therefore, and teach all nations, baptizing them in the name of the Father, and of the Son, and of the Holy Ghost, teaching them to observe all things whatsoever I have commanded you." (Matthew 28:19-20.)

I felt very sorry to leave Mr. Barton, as he was such a fine Christian, and a man whom I very highly esteemed.

A few days afterwards a very godly Baptist minister waited for me, and said that, having heard I had left the Evangelization Society, he had come to see if I would associate myself with his Church. I thanked him, and said I was going to trust the Lord, whose servant I was, to sustain me, and was not going to bind myself to any particular denomination. Many Christians thought I had made a mistake, but, thank God, I have never regretted the step then taken. I have had many deep trials, but the Lord has sustained and provided for me through them all.

I had a great desire, after leaving the Society, to labour in some out-of-the-way district, but did not intend to associate myself with those who are known as "brethren"; nor did I wish to be under the control of wealthy Christians, as my object was to throw myself entirely upon the Lord for both sustenance and guidance in His work.

I went to a little village in the County Londonderry, where the Gospel had seldom been preached. The Lord blessed the work there, and a dear old Christian woman supplied my temporal needs while in this place.

When there I had a most remarkable dream. I dreamed that I was going to an Orange Hall to preach the Gospel, and as I was about to enter a man came to me and said that the hall was full of people just waiting to hear how they might be saved. In my dream I looked up to the Lord and asked Him to give me the message for this congregation. The words in Revelation 3:8 came before me: "Behold, I set before thee an open door, and no man can shut it." I awoke, and on the same day I received a letter from Mr. William McLean, in which he said he had been to a place named Killeen (or, as it was sometimes called, "Sweet Killen that never saw Sunday"), and had preached in an Orange Hall, but could remain only one night.

He enquired if I could go, stating that if I did so I should find the hall filled with people sitting like little birds in a nest waiting and hungering for the Gospel, and that he felt sure that I should reap a rich harvest of souls for the Lord. I replied, saying I would go at once.

KILLEEN, 1878

I went, and on the first day about fifty were standing outside, unable to gain admission to the hall, as it was packed. Some of them caught hold of my coat and pushed their way in with me.

I took for my text the verse of my dream: "Behold, I set before thee an open door, and no man can shut it," but did not refer to my dream.

I had not been long speaking until many heads were bowed, and the cries of the anxious for mercy were heard coming from several parts of the building. I had to cease preaching because of the cries of those in distress about their souls, and we could scarcely get the meeting concluded.

I continued alone for almost a fortnight, the numbers and interest increasing nightly, and many passing from "death unto life."

I received a letter from Mr. McLean, in which he said that his arrangements for going to Liverpool had been cancelled, and that he felt inclined to come along and assist me. I was delighted to hear this, and wrote asking him to come immediately, saying, saying that the net was full and I was not able to get it to the shore.

This was the first time of our coming together in the work, and I found him to be a true yoke-fellow. We continued in this place for almost six months. The Spirit of the Lord moved greatly upon the people for miles around, and many were converted to God.

We instructed them in the doctrine of believers' baptism by immersion, which was quite a new thing to some, and caused much bitterness; though I had told them on the first night I preached that I was a baptised believer, and would immerse any true Christian who desired to follow the Lord in this Scriptural ordinance.

The first to be baptised was a man named James Henderson. I had been told that he wanted a little conversation with me on the subject. I went to him and enquired if he wished to speak to me on the question of baptism. "Not now," he replied, "I have been to the Word of God, and now I want to get to the water."

On a Lord's Day afternoon we baptised him in a river near by. Many people had heard of what we intended doing, and flocked across the country in large numbers, some cheering loudly; but when they came to the place and saw us going down into the water they were quite astonished: the cheering ceased, and many wept.

If Christians realised the solemnity of this ordinance and its signficance, they would lose no time in obeying the command; but, sad to say, some of the Lord's people join with the ungodly in turning it into ridicule.

We taught them to come together in the name of the Lord upon the first day of the week to remember Him in the breaking of bread, in accordance with the teaching of the Word of God; and a happy little company have been going on in that place for many years in this way.

We had some remarkable cases of conversion here, one of which was that of an old man who had been accustomed to lead in prayer in meetings for a number of years, and had often prayed with us at the commencement of our work, but the Lord opened his eyes and revealed to him that he had never been "born again." He acknowledged himself a guilty sinner before God, was converted, witnessed brightly for Christ during the short time he afterwards lived, and triumphantly passed away to be "forever with the Lord."

I was told one day of a woman who was believed to be dying. She had consulted a doctor, who had informed her that none of *his* medicines would do her any good. It was reported that she had been almost killed at the meetings. When I heard this I said that I had never known of anyone being killed at our meetings. I visited her, and found her sitting at the fire. "How do you feel?" I enquired. "I just feel as if I am going to drop into Hell," she replied.

I told her that she had been to the wrong physician, and that it was Christ she needed; and while I was speaking to her about the Saviour, she found peace through trusting in Him. There was nothing wrong with her body; she lived for a long time afterwards, rejoicing in the knowledge of sins forgiven.

On our way home from the meeting one night, a Scripture Reader of the Church of Ireland, who had attended many of our services, said to us that he could not understand how we were able to get up different subjects every night for months. "We do not get them up: we get them down," replied Mr. McLean.

One night, at the commencement of our meeting, I read the 8th chapter of Romans. When I came to

the words, "If any man have not the Spirit of Christ,
he is none of His", I paused, and told the people that
I felt impelled to read these words again. I did so,
and was constrained to repeat them a third time.

When we had finished preaching, and were going
amongst the anxious, an aged man caught hold of
Mr. McLean, saying Mr. Rea had passed him by and
he would not allow Mr. McLean to do so until he
had spoken to him. His face was wet with tears, and
he was trembling from head to foot under
conviction of sin. He told us he had been an Elder of
a Church for thirty-three years, and had held
family worship twice a day during all that time, but
he had never known he was on his way to Hell until
this night. While I had been reading the words, "If
any man have not the Spirit of Christ he is none of
His," he had been led to see that he had not the
Spirit of Christ. Mr. McLean sat down beside him,
and pointed him to the Saviour Who is both willing
and able to save, and in a short time the light of the
glorious Gospel shone into his soul, and the Spirit
witnessed with his spirit that he was born of God.
He immediately arose, and stretching out his hand
to his daughter, who had been brought to Christ a
few weeks previously, exclaimed, "Oh, my daughter,
I never knew I was on my way to Hell until tonight,
and now I know I am saved."

They both stood for some time weeping and
praising God, and many others were in tears at the
sight. When he reached home that night he said to
his wife, "We have been all wrong." This startled
her, but she came to the meetings also, and soon she,
too, was rejoicing in the knowledge of sins forgiven.

Chapter 6

MARKETHILL, 1878

In Markethill, which is a small town in County Armagh, we encountered much greater opposition than that related in any of the previous chapters.

We had much difficulty in securing a place in which to conduct our meetings, but at length succeeded in renting four upper rooms from an aged shoemaker, who was greatly addicted to drink.

On the first night the place was almost filled with a boisterous class of men, and on that evening, and for several nights aferwards, many of them kept on their hats: if anyone took his off some of the others put it on again, and shouted, "Why do you take your hat off to these fellows?" and altogether behaved so badly that I was on several occasions obliged to stop preaching and put some of them outside; although I was sometimes surprised at their allowing me to do so.

The windows were frequently broken with stones, and often the shoemaker and his companions were drinking and revelling downstairs while our meetings were going on above. Occasionally stones were thrown at us when passing along the streets, and the lady with whom we lodged, although a professed Christian, requested us to run past her house when we were being thus attacked.

Notwithstanding this, and amidst all the confusion, the Spirit of God worked mightily through the

Word preached, and several were brought to a saving knowledge of the Lord Jesus Christ.

We continued here a few weeks, and then left for a brief period. On the night of our departure Mr. McLean asked a young man if he were saved, or if he would like to be. With tears in his eyes he replied, "It's me who needs to be saved." He remained behind, and we sought to show him the ways of salvation. After we had been speaking to him a short time, Mr. McLean said, "We will now get down on our knees. What shall I say to God? Shall I ask Him to save you, or can we thank Him that He *has* saved you?" "Thank Him that He has saved me" was his reply.

We returned about eight days later, and on the night of our opening meeting we could scarcely get to the door, the place was so packed with people.

A man asked us if we remembered the young man who had professed conversion on the evening we left. We replied that we did. "Well," said he, "he died a few days afterwards, rejoicing in the Lord. He often spoke of the last night of the meeting in the room where God had saved him, and pleaded with all of us to meet him in the glory."

His testimony and death had an effect in the whole neighbourhood. Some of the more respectable people came afterwards to the meetings, and three in one family were brought to Christ.

A brother, speaking in the market-place a short time afer this, used the expression, "Friends, you have no tomorrow." A woman going to the pump for water heard the words, and they so impressed her that she crossed over to our landlady, who was standing at her door, and told her what the man had said. She answered, "Well, you should go and hear him out." She did so, and truly she had no tomorrow, for she died that night. I was informed that, through the words she heard, she had been led to trust the Saviour. How blessed it is to sow beside all waters—to be "instant in season and out of season"!

GLASGOW AND DUNDEE (FIRST VISIT), 1878

We then went to a large Conference of Christians in Glasgow, and afterwards took up Gospel work in the Marble Hall, Dumbarton Road, where we had a time of rich blessing. Several were brought to Christ, and the saints were revived. From this we went to Dundee, where the Lord also manifested His power through His Word. From Dundee I returned to Ireland.

FIRST TENT, BALLINDERRY, 1878

Before I left the Irish Evangelization Society, Mr. Barton asked me what I thought of tent-work for the North of Ireland. I said I believed it would be the right thing, as there were a number of places which could only be reached by such means.

On my return from Scotland I was greatly exercised as to getting a tent and, as I had no resource but God, I prayed earnestly that He would provide me with one.

Soon after this I had a letter from Mr. McLean in which he stated that Mr. Robert Stewart, of

Lisburn, had decided to supply us with a tent in which to preach the Gospel. To this honoured servant of God might be applied the words of inspiration, "After he had served his generation he fell on sleep." It has been clearly manifested that both he and his brother, Mr. James A. Stewart, were raised up by God in these remarkable days of Grace as bright witnesses for Him in the Gospel and amongst the saints.

When we obtained our tent, our first pitch was in Ballinderry. It was such a rare thing in that part that the people crowded to it from miles around. The Spirit of God began to work with great power, and within a few weeks quite a number professed faith in the Lord Jesus Christ. Some of these were notable sinners, and their testimony for God had a great effect upon the people in the district.

We taught them from the Scriptures believers' baptism and the breaking of bread on the first day of the week, and for years afterwards many assembled together here for this purpose.

On going out one morning we were astonished to find that our tent had been pulled down and badly damaged. This was, no doubt, the malicious work of those opposed to the Gospel.

When on our way to our lodgings one night, we were followed by a young woman who appeared to be in deep distress about her soul. Mr. McLean spoke to her and, while he was doing so, I had a most singular experience. I suddenly became overwhelmed with fear, and it seemed as if an audible voice said to me, "You are a hypocrite. You are preaching to others, although not yourself converted." I was in great anguish, and almost cried out in despair. Just then, however, Mr. McLean requested us to kneel in prayer; he commenced to pray, and I was in difficulty to know what to do. I felt impressed to follow him, but something seemed to prevent me. Still I was persuaded I ought to do so, and it was in this condition I began to pray. I had not continued long until the young woman was deeply affected, and cried out, "Oh, my sins, I am almost in Hell." I led on in prayer, and in a short time she exclaimed, "Praise God! I see Jesus. He has saved me," and as she found peace, the depression left me and I was filled with joy.

The lesson I learned from this experience was that the Lord permitted me to sink into despair, in order that I might be better able to give help and guidance to this young woman who was so burdened with her sins.

At one of our meetings a most unusual drowsiness came over the people; scarcely anyone seemed to be able to keep awake. I commenced to preach, but the sleepiness increased and, after speaking for a few minutes, I told them to go home and return the following night. Next night while I was praying at the commencement of the meeting, someone laughed outright, and I thought to myself, "It was a sleeping demon last night, but it is a laughing one tonight."

I sought guidance from the Lord, and prayed that, if my silence would be a blessing, I might refrain from preaching that night also. I then gave out a hymn and, whilst singing the second verse, an indescribable power fell upon the whole audience.

A man and his wife, who were sitting in one of the front seats, got down on their knees and cried aloud for mercy.

I was not permitted to preach that night, as the meeting seemed to be under the control of the Holy Spirit, and for several hours we were occupied in speaking to anxious souls. "His way is in the sea and His path is in the great waters, and His footsteps are not known."

Dear Mr. James Stewart, who had for years been laid aside through over-exertion in the great work of "fifty-nine" (he had been one of the leaders at that time), had his voice restored at one of our meetings, to the surprise and joy of all who knew him, and was enabled to go on in the service of the Lord, preaching the Gospel. "To God be the Praise and Glory."

When we left here Mr. James Stewart and Mr. W.J. Chapman continued the work, and a widow, who had been saved during our stay in this place, allowed them to conduct meetings in her house.

A man, whose wife had been converted at these services, was so enraged that one night about twelve o'clock he came, armed with a gun, and discharged a shot through one of the windows; but fortunately no person was injured, although some of the furniture in the room was damaged.

The matter was taken up by the authorities, who brought him to justice, and he was bound over to keep the peace for five years.

CARNMONEY, 1878

We left Ballinderry in the morning for Carnmoney, walking the whole way, which was almost twelve miles and, although it rained heavily for most part of the journey, we pitched our tent that same evening.

We got a cold reception at our lodgings—in fact no supper was prepared for us.

We remained here about three weeks, amidst a great deal of opposition and without any apparent results. The people seemed indifferent to the Gospel, and knew not the day of their visitation.

Chapter 7

DROMORE, COUNTY DOWN, 1878

After leaving Carnmoney we came to Dromore, where great opposition was shown to us from the very first. A well-known street orator was hired to preach against us, and for three successive nights he took his stand at our tent door, where a large crowd had congregated, to whom he lectured while our meetings were going on; but on the third night he became so intoxicated with drink and behaved so badly that the police were obliged to remove him to the barracks. Consequently he gave us no further trouble.

The power of God was soon manifested in the conviction and conversion of precious souls. We continued our meetings in the tent for about six weeks. Sometimes the numbers were so great we could scarcely gain admission, and on one occasion I had to crawl in under the canvas, as I found it impossible to get through the crowd standing around the door.

The season being advanced, we had to take our tent down but, as the interest was increasing—sixteen converts having been received into the assembly—we decided to continue our meetings, and for that purpose hired the Market House, which is in the centre of the town.

Our opening service was held on a Sunday evening. A short time before we commenced, the

Market House bell was set a-ringing, and a large crowd of rough-looking people speedily gathered, evidently expecting a disturbance, but we were not interfered with that evening.

I shall never forget the incidents which occurred on the following night; the place was crowded, and a large number of noisy and unruly people had congregated outside in the Market Square. When Mr. McLean had finished speaking, a man came forward and asked permission to lead in prayer. We had some doubts as to his object in this, but thought it better to allow him to do so. After uttering a few sentences he became confounded, and went away ashamed.

I then addressed the congregation and, while I was speaking, the mob outside (which by this time had increased until the number was about one thousand) had become furious. We saw that they were bent on mischief; they allowed all the women to go out, but prevented Mr. McLean, myself, and about twenty others from leaving the place.

What followed is indescribable; for about seven hours — from 9 p.m. until 4 a.m. — the conduct of the mob was diabolical. They began by breaking all the windows with stones, and we were obliged to take refuge under the seats. For the first three hours they made desperate efforts to force an entrance, but were unsuccessful. An Orangeman had, unknown to them, been closed in with us, and he became so enraged at their conduct that he determined to go out and fight his way through them, but he was almost killed in doing so.

I thought I would also venture out, but was

immediately attacked and very roughly handled,
being knocked down several times and trampled
upon. At length I managed to get upstairs again,
and a brother succeeded in helping me inside. A
Magistrate arrived upon the scene, but would do
nothing for us. There were also present four
policemen who made no attempt to come to our
assistance.

About midnight the crowd left the door for a few
minutes, and we took this opportunity to endeavour
to barricade it more securely, but they returned
with axes and broke it open, and for four hours
longer we were at their mercy, the publicans all the
time supplying them with drink. They dispersed
about four o'clock, and we were enabled to reach
the house of the brother with whom we had been
staying, where we found a number of Christians—
mostly women—who had assembled to pray for us.

After receiving some refreshments, we set out to
walk to Lisburn, which is ten miles from Dromore.
We were so worn-out that we had frequently to
rest on the way, and presented such an appearance
that the people going to the markets stopped to look
at us, evidently wondering who we were and where
we had been. My face was much bruised and
swollen; I had lost my hat, and was wearing an old
one which did not fit me well.

We arrived at the house of Mr. James Stewart,
Bow Street, Lisburn, at about eight o'clock in the
morning, and were met by Miss Fawcett (later Mrs.
Porter), who in a short time had breakfast prepared
for us, after partaking of which we felt greatly
revived. Many a Christian from both home and

abroad has been physically and spiritually refreshed at the house of Mr. Stewart.

On the following Sunday we returned to Dromore and commenced meetings in a large barn in the vicinity, owned by Mr. James Hamilton, which later became the birthplace of many souls, and where for several years afterwards a great work for God was carried on.

On the morning following the night of the uproar in the Market House, a man residing in the town, prompted by curiosity, went in to see the wreck, and before leaving the building he found peace through trusting Christ.

Several years afterwards Mr. McLean was preaching in a town in England. At the conclusion of one of his services, a man came to him and said, "You don't know me." "I do not," replied Mr. McLean. "Well," he said, "I was one of the men who led on the mob that night in Dromore to take your life. I fled to this country to escape being punished for the part I took in that wicked proceeding. I have since been saved, and am now in fellowship with the Christians here."

Mr. McLean enquired of one of the prominent members of the Assembly if this man were known to him, and he replied that he knew him well, and that he was a most consistent Christian. So that all the opposition shown in Dromore resulted in the furtherance of the Gospel and the conviction and conversion of sinners.

RANDALSTOWN, COUNTY ANTRIM, 1879

On the invitation of Mr. Roger Luke I visited Randalstown where I first met Mr. Halyburton who, being in a low state of health, had a short time previously come from Scotland in the hope that he might benefit by the change.

Before my arrival he held a few meetings, in which the power of God was so realised and the interest so great, that he decided to seek the aid of a fellow-labourer and continue the work in this place.

I united with him, and we commenced by holding a tea-meeting, which we called the "Sinners' Tea-Meeting." Free tickets of admission were distributed amongst the inhabitants of the district and, despite the unusual title, several hundreds responded to the invitation. Mr. Halyburton, Mr. McVicker, of Ballymena, and I preached the Gospel to them. The presence and power of God were greatly manifested, and many were under conviction of sin. The cries for mercy from the anxious reminded us of those scenes which occurred in "fifty-nine."

While here I had a nervous break-down, was unable to sleep, and had fits of acute depression. This I attributed to the reaction of the rough treatment which I had received in Dromore. I consulted a doctor who advised me to give up preaching altogether as the strain was too great for my nervous system. I was much troubled as to the right course to pursue, for I did not wish to leave the work; so I prayed to God that, if it were His mind that I should continue to preach, He would restore me to health again. A few days afterwards I fully recovered; my sleep returned, and I was able to enter vigorously into the work once more, and many were brought to Christ in this place.

Mr. Roger Luke, who was saved in 1859, related to me his conversion. He had been a giant in the service of Satan. Often in his native town four policemen found it difficult to take him to prison, and so outrageous was he when there that they were eventually obliged to secure him with a rope to a ring fixed into the wall of his cell; but in that memorable year of "fifty-nine" he was awakened to see his condition before God, and so great was his conviction of sin that he believed there was no mercy for him. He prayed to God to save his family, even if he should be lost. At last, in anguish of soul, he cried out, "Oh, Lord, if You will save me, You will never hear the end of it." God did save him; and in his house, where the Gospel has often been preached, many have passed from "death unto life."

Chapter 8

STRANDTOWN, BELFAST, 1879

Mr. C. Lepper, who was anxious that the Gospel should be preached in this district, secured a portion of ground for our tent, and invited us to pitch here. We had only been in this place about a fortnight, however, when our ground landlord sent four men, who hauled the tent down and placed it on the public highway.

Mr. Lepper succeeded in obtaining another field in the neighbourhood, and we again pitched here, but during our opening meeting we were surrounded by a hostile crowd, who hurled stones upon the canvas while the service was going on.

By the time the meeting was over the crowd had considerably increased, and their behaviour had become so bad that we saw they were bent on mischief.

Mr. and Mrs. Lepper and Mr. McLean went to their homes, but I concealed myself to see what would happen. I had not long to wait, as in a few minutes they commenced to cut the ropes of the tent, and when the watchman protested, they threatened to murder him if he interfered with them.

I came out from my hiding-place and when they saw me they all fled. I pursued them for almost half a mile, but was unable to overtake any of these enemies of the Gospel.

We left this place shortly afterwards, not having seen any blessing in this locality, the inhabitants of which were mostly Protestants.

HALF-PENNY GATE, MAZE, 1879

From Strandtown we went to the Half-Penny Gate, which is within a short distance of the Maze Race Course, where an annual horse race is held in the month of July.

We obtained ground for our tent, but were unable to secure lodgings for ourselves.

We felt convinced that God wished us to preach the Gospel to the people of this district, so we rented an empty barn, in which we placed a bed, a table, some seats, and a few cooking utensils. Some kind friends sent us victuals and, as Mr. McLean was a good cook and I could do housework very well, we got on happily together here.

Soon the Lord commenced to work in power, and many precious souls were saved through faith in the Lord Jesus Christ, some hardened and notable sinners being convicted of sin and converted to God.

We, as usual, taught the converts Believers' Baptism and the truth of gathering together upon the first day of the week to remember the Lord in the breaking of bread, so that in the very room, or barn, which we had had so much difficulty in procuring, a goodly number of the Lord's people, most of whom were saved during the time of our mission, assembled for many years afterwards to

worship Him on the Lord's Day, in accordance with
the teaching of Scripture.

Messrs. James Stewart and W.J. Chapman, of
Lisburn, carried on the work after we left. While
here Mr. McLean took suddenly ill, and was laid
aside for a long time.

KILLYKERGAN, COUNTY DERRY, 1879-1880

A brother invited me to Killykergan to conduct a
series of Gospel meetings in a new hall which had
been built in this place. I went, and held my first
service on the memorable night of the Tay Bridge
disaster, Sunday, December 28th, 1879. Many of
thet inhabitants of the district were greatly
prejudiced against those who supported the work in
the hall, and I preached nightly for two weeks
without seeing any visible manifestation of blessing.
I became exercised about this, and prayed fervently
that the Lord would give me some token of His
presence and power, if it were His will that I should
continue the mission.

That same night, at the close of the meeting, a
young woman told me that she had been saved a
few nights previously, and I looked upon this as a
direct answer to prayer and an evidence that the
Lord wished me to remain here a little longer.

The following night was one of great blessing;
many were brought under conviction of sin, and for
a few nights afterwards we enjoyed much of the
presence of the Lord. But Satan, who is always
seeking an opportunity to hinder the work of God,
soon began to manifest his power through one

whom we had considered a Christian, but who then proved himself to be a man who was in the gall of bitterness.

How true the words of the Lord Jesus, "Not that I am come to send peace on the earth; I came not to send peace, but a sword" (Matthew 10:34). And again, "I am come to send fire on the earth, and what if it be already kindled?" (Luke 12:4).

When the Gospel is preached in power, opposition in some shape or form is inevitably shown. In this instance its opponent was a man who for several years had taken his place at the Lord's Table, although some believed he had been deceived and had not been truly "born again."

For several weeks I thought him my best friend, but suddenly he became my greatest enemy, saying that if what I preached were true, then he was not a Christian at all. So acute was his opposition that one night about eleven o'clock I was obliged to leave my lodgings and walk to a village situated about two miles distant, where I obtained sleeping accommodation in the house of a Roman Catholic.

When I arrived at the hall on the following night it was packed with people, and many were standing outside, unable to gain admission. I held my meeting, and immediately I had finished speaking, my opponent stood up and publicly denounced me, saying, that as he had the key of the hall, he would lock the door and thus prevent my having any further meetings there.

The confusion which followed this statement amounted almost to a panic. My friends, who were much distressed, resented this high-handed action;

while the enemies of the Gospel rejoiced at his treatment of me.

I felt saddened to think that the hall should be closed against me, especially as the attendance was so large and I had had such liberty in the proclamation of the Gospel.

A Mr. Robinson, however, of the same district, opened his house for meetings, the Lord blessed us greatly, and most of Mr. Robinson's family were saved during the time I was with him.

GARVAGH, 1880

In this place I hired what was formerly called a "chapel of ease," but I found it anything but a chapel of ease to me. The enemies of the Gospel used every means in their power to prevent my coming to this town. The spiritual darkness was great for it is still true that men love darkness rather than light.

I was unable to secure lodgings in a Protestant house, but a nice Roman Catholic family, which consisted of a widow, her son, and four grown-up daughters, let me have some apartments. They were very kind and sociable, and did everything to make me comfortable. I prayed and sang hymns, and had often most interesting conversations with them regarding eternal things.

On one occasion one of the daughters said to me, "I do not think there is any difference between you and us, as the clergymen of the town are all against you, and the priest will not visit our house since you came." I replied that there was no difference whatever, if she were "born again."

Very few attended my first meeting, but I had previously been told not to be surprised at this, as the people had been warned that an attack was to be made upon me that night. A hostile crowd gathered outside and threw stones into the building but, fortunately, no one was hurt.

I expected to be attacked on my way to my lodgings but, thank God, I arrived there uninjured. The few friends, however, who followed me were set upon by the mob and stoned, some being severely hurt. It was a very dark night, and this served as a protection for me, as I had gone on alone in advance of my friends. The following night four policemen guarded me home, a man carrying a lantern walking behind, and a mob on either side, ready to assault me, if an opportunity offered. The Lord, however, preserved me from harm, and I was able to continue here for several weeks.

The meetings increased in numbers, better order prevailed, and many were convicted of sin and converted to God. One woman, who was reported to have been the worst character in the town, was saved during this mission. In a river near by I baptised six converts, one of whom was the daughter of a clergyman.

A man had threatened to shoot me if I dared to immerse any one in this locality, and, while the baptism was taking place, he came armed with a gun and concealed himself adjacent to the river-bank, but the Lord prevented him from carrying out his threat.

Chapter 9

LAURELVALE, 1880

Laurelvale is a small village in the County Armagh, and is situated about three miles from the place where I was born. I pitched my tent here, and continued meetings for ten weeks. Many professed conversion during these meetings, and a number were baptised publicly in the presence of more than three hundred spectators, who stood on the river bank witnessing the ordinance. While we were singing a hymn at the close of one of our services, a young man was deeply impressed with the words of the last verse:—

> "O ye, who now salvation spurn,
> Oh, dreadful thought, in hell to burn!
> Never to come back any more:
> Oh, no, no, never to come back any more."

Some time afterwards he went to America, where he remained for several years, but the words, "Oh, dreadful thought—in hell to burn," kept recurring to his mind.

On one occasion a number of men were killed at his side by an accident. The words of the hymn were brought more vividly before him, and caused him such anxiety of soul that he began to give his money to the poor, in the hope of easing his conscience by this means. He had no peace, however, as the words, "Oh, dreadful thought—in hell to burn," rang louder and louder in his ears. He became so depressed that he was unable to attend to his work, and decided to return home to Ireland and find out, if possible, the way of salvation.

Shortly after reaching his native town, he came into contact with a young man whom he had known from boyhood, and who had been converted during the time he was away. While they were conversing together, his friend spoke to him about his soul, and pointed him to the Saviour Who is ever ready and willing to save all that come unto God by Him, the "light of the glorious Gospel" shone into his heart, and he was there and then led to trust Christ.

RICHHILL, 1880

Mr. McLean, having recovered from a prolonged illness, united with me again in the work; and after leaving Laurelvale we pitched in Richhill, which is a small town in the County Armagh, about six miles from Portadown. While we were thus engaged, a lad enquired of us what time the circus commenced. "At seven o'clock tomorrow night," I replied, and invited him to come to it. We continued here for fourteen weeks, the attendance being so great that often large numbers were unable to gain admission.

We had some very singular cases of conversion here, one of which was that of Miss Maggie Ballantyne. She had been under conviction of sin for a long time and, although I had often spoken to her about her soul, she was unable to grasp the truth of "justification by faith."

One night at the close of the meeting I read to her
Isaiah 53:6 in the following manner:— "All we like
sheep have gone astray." "Do you believe that
sentence?" I asked her. "I do," she replied, and
added, "That's what troubles me." I then read the
second clause, "We have turned every one to his
own way," and repeated my question. She again
replied, "I do." "And the Lord hath laid on Him the
iniquity of us all," I continued. "Do you believe
that?" I again enquired. She remained perfectly
silent. I wished her good-night, and she left the
tent.

The following day, while she was sitting in her
garden pondering on the verse, the Spirit of God
revealed to her that Christ had borne all her sins,
and that she had only to believe the last clause of the
verse as she did the first.

She immediately ran into the house and told her
parents that she was saved, and soon they and
several of the neighbours who had assembled
united in praising God for her salvation.

I have never met a more consistent Christian
than she. She had such a tender conscience and was
so artless that we named her "The Baby of the
Assembly." I baptised her and another sister one
winter's evening, after having to break the ice
which covered the water.

For three years she witnessed brightly for Christ,
but one Saturday night she took suddenly ill and, on
the following Sunday week, passed away "to be
forever with the Lord."

Although sometimes in great pain, she spent her

last day on earth in speaking about Christ to the friends and neighbours who had come to see her, warning the unsaved to "flee from the wrath to come," and exhorting the Christians to witness for the Lord on every opportunity.

Her face beamed with joy, and even after death her countenance retained its expression of triumphant rapture.

I spent two hours with her on the day of her home-call. She requested me to preach at her funeral, asking me to take for my text Isaiah 53:6, through which she had been saved and I readily promised to do so.

I conducted the service at the house and also at the graveside, and preached at both places from the words of the verse, "All we like sheep have gone astray, we have turned every one to his own way, and the Lord hath laid on Him the iniquity of us all."

Her brother-in-law, who was unconverted and indeed almost an infidel, and who could never be induced to attend any of our meetings, was present at the funeral. He was convicted of sin at the graveside, and a short time afterwards he also was led to trust Christ through the words of this much-used verse of Scripture.

Billy Pressick was another bright case who was converted at these meetings. He had been a notorious sinner; his appearance was anything but prepossessing, and his language anything but refined. He seemed such a hopeless case, and was so antagonistic towards the things of God that I thought it almost impossible to reach him with the Gospel, and on one occasion, after we had had a conversation with him, I said to Mr. McLean, "Do you think that God could save that man?"

But, oh, what a change when next we saw him, which was about a week afterwards. Billy had been truly saved, and was as mild as a lamb and, instead of oaths and curses which had hitherto issued from his mouth, there were praises and thanksgivings to God for saving such a sinner as he.

He was by occupation a ploughman, and employed by a farmer who was strongly opposed to us, and who made no profession of Christianity whatever; yet the farmer stated there must be something in this "conversion" when it could make such a change in a man as it had done in Billy Pressick.

He was a heavy smoker, but one day when ploughing he laid his pipe down in front of the plough, saying, "I am now going to bury you, and there is never to be a resurrection."

A man on one occasion invited him into a public-house. "I cannot go," said he, "for there is another with me." "Bring him in, too," said the man. "He wouldn't come," replied Billy. "Who is he?" enquired he. "The Lord Jesus Christ," answered Billy.

Billy's reason for refusing to enter one of these sinful rendezvous was much better than a pledge or a "blue ribbon," as it was a testimony to the keeping power of the Lord Jesus, as well as to His saving grace.

We taught the converts "Believers' Baptism," and before we left about seventy were gathered together to remember the Lord in the breaking of bread upon the first day of the week; and sometimes we found it difficult to bring these

Lord's Day morning meetings to a close, as we realised His presence so much, and the fellowship of the saints was so sweet.

Chapter 10

AHOREY, COUNTY ARMAGH, 1880-1881

The tent season being over, we commenced meetings in a house in this district. The Lord blessed us greatly, and many professed faith in Christ.

One night when I ascended the platform I had a most singular experience. I tried to address my audience, but could command no language to do so. I thereupon told the people that we must pray to God for help to enable me to conduct the meeting. We prayed for some time, and I again mounted the platform but I was quite dumbfounded and could not utter a word: so I dismissed the meeting.

The news of this strange occurrence spread throughout the country, and on the following night a large number of strangers came to see the "dumb preacher," as they now called me; but the Lord afterwards gave me great liberty and so manifested His power that within a few nights several had passed from "death unto life."

This place has been a centre of great blessing for many years. We commenced a Believers' Fellowship meeting on the 12th July, and Conferences of Believers have been held here annually on that date ever since. The Lord has greatly blessed these gatherings, which sometimes number upwards of five hundred, who spend the day in happy fellowship, listening to the ministry of the Word of God.

Mr. Williamson, on whose grounds the Assembly Room is built, has been for many years identified with this work, and has always given a warm welcome to all of the Lord's people attending these Conferences.

HAMILTONSBAWN, 1881

This is a small village in the County Armagh, situated about three miles from the town of Markethill. We pitched our tent here early in the summer, and very soon saw manifestations of the power of God in the convicting and converting of sinners. The attendance increased until we had scarcely standing room. On one occasion at the close of our meeting, five people in different parts of the tent fell upon their knees, each calling upon the Lord for salvation.

An incident happened here which might have had serious consequences, had not the Lord in His grace intervened. A party of about sixty men had, unknown to us, conspired to come on a certain night and upset our meeting. About the same number of men who, although unconverted, sympathised with us, heard of the plot, and armed themselves with weapons, which they concealed. Both parties met outside the tent door, but our intended assailants were overawed and, except for a slight scuffle between the two parties, nothing serious occurred.

We thanked God that nothing disastrous took place, for had the different elements come into conflict, no doubt many would have been injured.

About this time I had a severe trial. My eldest son, a boy aged fourteen years, died. He had for a long time been in a delicate state of health, and we were very anxious about him—both spiritually and temporally. The evening following his conversion I, not knowing that he had professed faith in Christ, said to him, "What about your soul now, William Henry?" He smiled, and replied, "I am saved." I was greatly surprised at his answer, and said, "Is it really true?" "I have no doubt about it," he replied.

I asked him if any particular Scripture had led to his conversion. "No," he answered, and added, "I just saw that Christ had died for me, and that through His work on the Cross my sins were all put away." I called his mother into the room, and we knelt down together and thanked the Lord for saving our boy. Indeed, I did not cease praising Him for several hours.

About three months afterwards, his health having somewhat improved, he was received into fellowship with the Lord's people, and continued to meet with them while his health permitted. He had a deep knowledge of the Scriptures and a keen desire for the Word of God, and there was scarcely an incident or story in the Bible with which he was not familiar.

After a short time, however, he had a relapse, and the doctor, on examining him, said to me, "I have very little hope of his recovery." I told him the doctor's opinion, and he smilingly answered, "I am ready to go."

He lingered for almost six months, but no

murmur escaped his lips; he seemed happy at the thought of his release, and often spoke of it with calmness and joy.

About a week before his departure he asked me to pray that the Lord, if it were His will, would take him home that night.

A few days before he died, while sitting by his bedside I saw that he looked troubled. I asked him if he had any doubts as to his safety in Christ. "Oh, there are doubts," he replied. I then perceived that the "enemy of souls" was at work upon the weak boy.

I read some appropriate portions of the Word of God to him, and prayed, after which he said, "Isn't it *true* that the 'blood of Jesus Christ His Son cleanseth us from all sin'?" "Praise God," I exclaimed, "You have got the victory. 'They overcame him by the blood of the Lamb'." His face brightened, and he said, "Thank God. Satan may now go."

Never, since the night I was saved, was the blood of Christ more precious to me than on that occasion. I could not help saying, "What a mean enemy the devil is, to so attack a poor weak boy in his last hours."

After this he had a time of great peace and joy, and seemed to forget all his suffering. On the following Thursday afternoon a great change took place. The intense pain which he had been suffering ceased. A sister in the Lord, who was in the room, said, "William Henry, won't you be glad to see Jesus?" An expression of heavenly joy overspread his face, and in a strong, clear voice, he replied, "I think I will. I shall soon see Him."

Shortly afterwards I said to him, "Isn't that a lovely hymn we used to sing together?" and repeated the first two lines:—

"I know there is a bright and a glorious land,
    Away in the heavens high,"

but he interrupted me, saying, "Father, there is a better verse than that. It is 'the blood of Jesus Christ His Son cleanseth us from all sin'," and added, "You remember the other evening when Satan had to fly."

Seeing us all weeping around him, he asked, "Why do you weep? Is it because I'm soon to be in the Glory?" These were his last words. He quietly "fell asleep in Jesus", without a struggle and apparently without pain — just as the summer's sun was setting at the close of a bright day in the month of July, 1881.

"Precious in the sight of the Lord is the death of His saints."

LOUGHGALL, COUNTY ARMAGH, 1881

Having heard that this was a very irreligious village, we decided to pitch our tent somewhere in its vicinity, and consulted a man regarding the renting of a piece of ground at Orr's Turn.

He advised us to pitch at a place about a mile further on, where the inhabitants were reputed to be more religiously inclined. Many good men, he stated, during the past fifty years had attempted to preach to the people at Orr's Turn, but no good results had been obtained. We told him that the greater the sinner the greater his need of the Gospel, and that Jesus Christ Himself said, "I came not to call the righteous, but sinners to repentance." From our conversation with him we concluded that this was exactly the place for us to pitch.

We obtained the ground, and soon had our tent erected. The people came in such numbers that often a crowd was standing around the door, unable to get inside.

Towards the end of the season Mr. McLean's health again gave way, and he was reluctantly obliged to discontinue the work. I obtained great assistance, however, from Mr. James Stewart, of Lisburn, who came as often as he could.

We visited throughout the country during the day, had access into almost every house, and were gladly welcomed by the people, who listened attentively while we talked to them of the "things of God."

In our visiting, one day we knocked at the door of a neat little cottage, which was opened by a most respectable-looking lady. I inquired of her if God were in this house. "No," she candidly replied, "God is not in this house." "It must, indeed, be a miserable house where God is not," said I.

She invited us inside, and before we left, we asked her to come to our tent meetings. She came the same night, accompanied by her daughter, and a week afterwards they were both rejoicing in the knowledge of sins forgiven.

The interest was so great that we continued our meetings in the tent until late in the autumn. It was, however, eventually blown down during a severe storm, but we secured a large store from Mr. Orr, and held a few further meetings in it.

Our last day at Orr's Turn was a memorable one. I preached that morning at Hamiltonsbawn, after which I walked two miles to the Assembly Room at Richhill, and there met with the Christians to remember the Lord in the breaking of bread.

In the afternoon about one hundred of us marched six miles to Mrs. Murray's schoolroom at Cranagill, singing praises to God all the way. I addressed a meeting there at four o'clock, after which I and about four hundred others walked to Orr's Turn, again singing *en route*. When we arrived, we found the meeting-place packed with people, the storeyard and the adjacent houses also being filled.

I preached in the large store to an audience numbering over seven hundred. After I had spoken for almost an hour I asked them to retire so that those outside could get in, but not one of them would leave; so I took my stand at the top of the stairs and preached to the huge crowd in the yard below.

During this time a young man was addressing a meeting in a smaller store in another part of the building, and it also was packed with people. Our audience must have numbered at least sixteen hundred persons, some women among them having walked twelve miles to attend the meeting. Truly the harvest was great, but the labourers were few.

I felt so exhausted that night that I thought my health would break down, but the Lord strengthened me, and I was enabled to continue for the greater part of the winter, preaching in Mrs. Murray's schoolroom, where I had been invited to conduct services.

The attendance here on week-nights was very large, and on Sunday evenings the place was filled two hours before the time appointed to commence.

Mr. Stewart occasionally conducted the services, and one Sunday, while spending the day with Mr. Dunlop, he said he would like to retire for an hour's quietness before going to the meeting. "We should now be at the school-house," answered Mr. Dunlop. "But it is yet two hours until the time," said Mr. Stewart. "I know that," he replied, "but you will find some difficulty in getting in, even if we leave now."

When they arrived the crowd was so great that they could scarcely get near the door. After many vain attempts to force their way through, someone called out Mr. Stewart's name and requested the people to make way for him, and at length with great difficulty he succeeded in reaching the platform, but it was also crowded.

Eventually a little space was cleared, and he was able to open the meeting, but in a short time the heaviness of the atmosphere extinguished the lights. After re-lighting them, and giving the room a little more ventilation, he continued for almost an hour. At the close a hymn was sung, and he intimated that the service was now over, but no one made any attempt to leave.

He again commenced, preached for a further half-hour, closed with prayer, and asked the people to retire, but still they remained. He gave out another hymn, and when it was sung, a few began to move slowly out, and at last the congregation dispersed, some having been in the building for over four hours. Such was the thirst for the Word of God at this time.

A large number were brought to Christ at these meetings, many of the well-to-do people of the district being among the converts.

Chapter 11

CLARE, COUNTY ARMAGH, 1882

This is a district within a short distance of Tandragee. Mrs. White, a Christian lady of the latter place, who had a great desire for the salvation of souls, told me of a large barn which could be hired for the preaching of the Gospel. I rented it for three months, at the moderate charge of ten shillings.

It was a large building, and seated about six hundred people. We did not expect a big attendance as the district was very thinly populated, but in less than a week we were surprised to find that we had not sufficient room to accommodate the numbers who came.

Many were men who had always been taught that it was impossible for any person to know if he were saved until he appeared before the Judgment Seat of Christ. They listened very attentively, however, while I preached the Gospel in its simplicity, showing them "justification by faith in the Lord Jesus Christ," and pointing out to them that, "By grace are ye saved through faith, and that not of yourselves: it is the gift of God" (Ephesians 2:8), and that only those who were "born again" would ever see the Kingdom of God.

When I had been here for about six weeks, it was suggested that we should have a Gospel tea-meeting. This I agreed to, and, having made the necessary arrangements, I announced that a free tea would be given, and we extended a hearty invitation to all.

The numbers who came far exceeded our expectations and, although we had £11 worth of food and a boiler which contained sixty gallons of tea, our provisions were far short of our requirements.

We had int nded, after tea, to deliver short Gospel addresses to the congregation, and had invited a few brethren to take part, but when we were just about to commence our service, someone raised the cry of "Fire," and immediately a fearful panic ensued.

The scene which followed is beyond description. Some jumped fourteen feet on to a hard pavement, others burst open a trapdoor which led to an apartment below, and many fell through it. Fortunately, the Lord preserved life and, with the exception of one old lady whose leg was slightly injured, no one was hurt.

Just about the time of the uproar, Mr. Archibald Bell, who resided ten miles distant, was constrained to pray that the Lord would that night preserve us from harm. He was surprised next day to learn of this incident, and thanked God for answering prayer.

The alarm of fire was false, some evil-disposed person having raised it, but we never discovered who it was. Some of those present charged me with being the indirect cause of the calamity, and several threatened to maltreat me, and vowed they would kill me if I came back again.

I returned, however, on the following Lord's

Day, and found the barn crowded and many people standing outside, unable to obtain an entrance. The Lord over-ruled and, despite the threats of the previous night, no violence was shown me, and I conducted my meeting undisturbed; although in some of my later meetings occasional outbursts of opposition were displayed.

On one occasion my opponents invited a clergyman to attend one of my services, evidently expecting him to contradict me. He came on a Sunday evening and as I was entering the building I was informed of his presence and requested to ask him to speak, but as he was not known to me, I did not care to do so.

I conducted the service, and at the close he came forward and said to me that he would like to speak a word for God to these people. I replied that I would gladly give him the opportunity.

He began by saying: "I am a Presbyterian minister, but I do not believe that the 'laying on of hands' by an Presbytery can confer the gift of preaching upon any man. I believe in a God-sent and God-commissioned preacher, and I am glad to stand by my brother here tonight in the support of his mission for the proclamation of the Gospel of our Lord and Saviour Jesus Christ." He first addressed those who knew their sins forgiven, and stated that he was one of those who "had passed from death unto life."

He then spoke to the unsaved, and told them that there was no safety except in the precious blood of the Lamb of God which taketh away the sin of the world; and for about fifteen minutes he delivered a very solemn Gospel address.

A few of the elders of his Church were much displeased at his words, and used strong language regarding him; but, nevertheless, his address had a very telling effect upon the people, and broke down much of the prejudice that had been manifested towards me.

With the occasional assistance of Mr. James Stewart and a few other friends, I carried on the meetings in this place for twenty successive weeks, preaching every week-night and three or four times on Sunday.

Hundreds of people in this district, who a short time previously had been living careless lives, indifferent to the things of God, when I left were thirsting for the Word of Life.

CLONMAIN, LOUGHGALL, 1882

The tent season had now having arrived and, as I had obtained a new tent which seated eight hundred people, I resolved to visit Loughgall again, and secured ground at a place called Clonmain, which is a short distance from where I had been the year previous.

Many were saved at these meetings, but as a large number had been converted on my former visit, I devoted some of my addresses to the teaching of Christians in the doctrines of "Believers' Baptism" and the gathering together upon the first day of the week to remember the Lord in the breaking of bread.

In those days it was no light matter to teach the whole Truth of God, especially doctrines which were vigorously opposed by eminent religious leaders; indeed many clergymen publicly denounced me from their pulpits. This prejudiced some against me, but caused others to search the Scriptures more diligently that they might learn the right course to pursue, and on one occasion, after an address to Christians, I baptised twenty Believers. These, with several others, gathered together to remember the Lord on the first day of the week, our numbers increasing until sixty were in fellowship in the little assembly.

It was beautiful to hear these young men, with hearts full of the praises of God, testifying to His saving and keeping power, and encouraging one another in the "ways of the Lord."

Their testimony has been a blessing in the district, and the Lord has raised up many from amongst them to preach the Gospel and minister His Word, to the edification of the saints.

One young man, who had a real shepherd's heart, was soon taken home. His death was much felt by the Christians. Before he passed away he requested that I should preach at his funeral, but the officials of the Church to which his parents belonged refused to allow them to bury him in the family burying-ground unless they promised that I should not preach at the graveside. This his mother, however, declined to do, and they were obliged to obtain burying-ground in another church-yard. As the funeral procession was about to start, a message was received from the clergyman of the Church to which we were going that I would not be allowed to conduct the funeral service, or even permitted to enter the graveyard.

I knew he had no legal authority to hinder me; so I told the messenger to inform him that, unless he had a guard of police with fixed bayonets to prevent me, I would go into the graveyard and preach at the graveside. The Christians who attended the funeral were very much perplexed, not knowing what turn events would take.

When we arrived at the church gates, contrary to my expectations, no one interfered with me, but while at the graveside, after we had sung the hymn, "Safe in the Arms of Jesus," and just as I commenced to pray, the clergyman came running towards us, shouting, "Ye villains, get out of this," and during all the time I was praying he raved at us like a madman. With the exception of the grave-digger's wife, who ordered her husband to leave, no one paid any attention to him whatever, and the old grave-digger "stuck to his post."

After prayer, I read some appropriate Scriptures, from which I preached the Gospel. The presence and power of God was felt, and many tears were shed by those present, whose hearts the Word of God had touched. In a short time the clergyman left, not one of the company having spoken a word to him. Some of his own people were highly displeased at his conduct, and from my heart I thanked God that I was not under the power of an ecclesiastical Government.

ELEVEN-LANE-ENDS, 1882

This is a rural district in the County of Armagh,

and a short distance from Tandragee. I came here on the invitation of a man who had several years previously invited me to preach at his place, but on my arrival he declined to allow me to commence meetings, stating that, if he did so, his house might be burned.

Strange to say that, although he had again invited me, when I arrived with my tent he refused to allow me to pitch it upon his ground, still fearing that he would suffer some injury should I do so.

While he and I were discussing the matter, I observed two men in a field, just opposite his house, engaged in brick-making. I went over and asked them if they would accept two pounds (£2) for ground in this field, upon which to pitch my tent for the season. One of them replied that he would, and very soon I had my tent erected — just opposite my fickle friend's door.

Contrary to his forebodings, we were not molested during the whole period that we remained here, although he made several attempts to raise opposition against me, and on one occasion I had to order him to leave the tent.

The people attended the meetings in hundreds, and I have never seen a more noble and kind community anywhere than the inhabitants of Eleven-Lane-Ends.

I continued here for fourteen weeks, the attendance increasing until I sometimes saw almost one thousand people packed in my tent, while about two hundred were standing outside.

The Lord blessed us greatly in the awakening of sinners, and many were brought to a saving knowledge of the Truth.

The last meeting was held in the open field, my tent having been blown down a few hours previously, during a terrific storm which had raged throughout the day.

Chapter 12

ENGLAND

Barnstaple, Bath, Bristol, Hereford, Leominster, London, and Stroud, 1882

After storing my tent for the winter, I went to Leominster Conference, and from thence to Barnstaple, where Messrs. Chapman and Hake had kindly invited me to spend a few days, thinking that after my arduous labours in the tent I required a little rest. I spent ten days with them, and still have fond recollections of the sweet fellowship which we had together.

I also visited Bath, Hereford, Stroud, and Bristol. I had a very refreshing time in Stroud. The Christians were moving into a new hall, and they asked me to open it with a series of Gospel meetings. I did so, and from the commencement the Lord's presence was felt in the place.

A young woman, after attending one of the meetings, was so troubled about her soul that when she arrived at her home, and supper was offered to her, she said: "No, I'll not eat, drink, nor sleep until my soul is saved." And she did not, for at two o'clock on the following morning the "light of the glorious Gospel" shone in upon her, and she was born of God. Several others were saved in the hall on the same night.

While in Bristol I visited Mr. Müller's Homes, and

one morning preached to five or six hundred of the
orphans at breakfast-time. I thank God for having
raised up such a man as Mr. Müller, and for
sustaining his faith in the face of so many
difficulties.

From Bristol I went to London, and there in
Clapton Hall gave a short account of the Lord's
work in Ireland.

BANBRIDGE, 1883

I commenced tent-work here in the beginning of
April, and continued it for six weeks. The Lord
blessed the Word preached, and a few were brought
to Christ.

DONACLONEY, 1883

This is a small village in the County Down,
situated about four miles from Lurgan. Mr. Liddell
kindly gave me ground for the tent, adjacent to his
factory gate.

I was subjected here to the taunts and sneers of
some of the villagers, who scoffed at me as I passed
in and out of the tent, but otherwise no opposition
was shown; and although it was a little humiliating
to the flesh to be jeered at, yet I rejoiced that I was
called upon to suffer shame for His Name's sake.

There were some bright cases of conversion here,
although not so many as I have sometimes seen in
other places where I laboured.

GARRETROSS, 1883

On leaving Donacloney, I pitched the tent at Garretross, but the attendance was very small, and all efforts to reach the people were treated with indifference. Nevertheless, a few were saved. "To God be all the glory."

At the close of one of the services, which had been conducted by Mr. James Stewart, a man, aged about seventy years, said to him, "I have lost fifty years of religion tonight." He was an exemplary man in the neighbourhood and most upright in all his dealings, yet he found out that he was a sinner, and required to be born again before he could see the Kingdom of God.

KILLYMAN, 1883

This is a parish in the Counties of Armagh and Tyrone, and stretches to within three miles of Dungannon.

On the day that I secured the ground for the tent here I visited a house and read and prayed with the family, but so unusual was this occurrence that they reported that a man astray in the mind was going about the country.

On returning a few days later with my tent, I found the house of the lady who had given me the ground shut up.

I commenced to erect the tent on the ground chosen, but had not been long engaged in this work when a man came to me and said, "What are you going to do?" "I am going to put up a tent," I replied.

"I don't think you are," he retorted. "Who gave you
the authority?" I informed him that I had got the
ground from the lady of the house. After a little
further conversation he asked me in a very serious
tone, "Are you the Holy Fathers?" "Oh, no," I
replied, "I have not got that length yet." "Oh, then,"
he said, "go on, and I will help you up with it."

I encountered great opposition here, largely
through a clergyman who denounced me from the
pulpit and circulated printed leaflets advising the
people not to attend my meetings, as I did not
believe in repentance or prayer.

One day he entered the house of a woman who
had been brought to Christ at the meetings and,
after reproving her for attending them, said, "Do
you not know that they are Plymouth Brethren?"
"Oh, no, they can't be 'Plymouth Brethren'," said
she. "But they *are*," replied he. "Well," said she, "the
first night I went to hear him the preacher spoke on
repentance and showed the necessity of it, and the
leaflets you sent state that the Plymouth Brethren
don't believe in repentance. The second meeting I
went to he exhorted the Christians to pray, and the
leaflet says they don't believe in prayer."

Some time afterwards a number of this clergyman's supporters conspired to assemble on a certain
night and destroy the tent. The police, however,
heard of their intention, and intercepted them
while on their way to perpetrate this dastardly
deed, and during the entire night guarded the tent
from harm.

Notwithstanding all the opposition shown, and
the slanderous statements circulated, the Lord

manifested His power in the conversion of a goodly number in this district.

I continued here until the end of the tent season, and before leaving publicly baptised several of the converts in a river in the vicinity.

A number of men came to the river bank with the intention of preventing my carrying out this solemn ordinance, but the Lord so confounded them that they stood by and silently looked on without attempting to interfere with us.

On returning, after the baptism, to my lodgings I found my landlady weeping bitterly. "I never thought I should see anything like this in this country," she told me, "and I'll not be surprised if they kill you yet before you leave."

I replied that the Killyman Protestants might fight and defeat Home Rule, but they would find it more difficult to overcome the Lord's servants.

The season now being over, I took my tent down and stored it past for the winter.

Chapter 13

NORWOOD, LONDON, 1883

A gentleman invited me here to conduct a series of Gospel meetings. I felt sorry to see so many Christians in this place apparently regardless as to their associations with the world in its religious formalities and evil doctrines.

I went one day to what was termed a "Union Prayer Meeting." One of the speakers, in giving his opinion as to how far Christian love and fellowship should extend, mentioned that he had been speaking to a lady who had stated that she would draw the line of separation at Unitarianism. "But," said he, "I would not draw the line even there."

When he had finished speaking a well-known evangelist was called upon to pray, and I was surprised to hear him do so, as if all the corrupt doctrines endorsed in the previous address were taught in the Word of God, especially Unitarianism, which holds that the Lord Jesus Christ was only a good man, and not the Incarnate Son of God.

My soul was longing for an opportunity to witness for my absent Lord, and when he had concluded I led in prayer, and heartily asked God to deliver us from all damnable heresies, including Unitarianism, which so belittles the precious blood of the Christ of God Who bore our sins in His own body on the tree.

I felt more determined than ever to declare the

whole counsel of God while in this district, and the Lord so blessed the testimony that before I left eighteen had followed Him in baptism.

At these baptisms the Lord manifested His presence, and it was gloriously blessed to see rich and poor go down into the "waters of baptism" together.

On the invitation of Mr. Mandeville, I visited Tring, where we had a season of rich blessing. Several were brought to the Lord, and at the close of the mission sixteen were baptised; amongst these were a coachman and a gardener of the Messrs. Rothchild. Mr. Mandeville baptised them, and a solemn awe pervaded the meeting. I believe, if convenient, all baptisms should be public.

ISLE OF MAN, 1884

It had for a long time been impressed upon my mind that I should work my tent for a season in the Isle of Man; so, having made all the necessary arrangements, I shipped from Belfast and landed there the following morning with my tent.

I secured ground for it in the town of Laxey, and had the carts engaged to convey it there, when I took suddenly ill, and was unable to get the tent pitched. I awoke about twelve o'clock that night, and felt so ill that I thought I must be dying; and, being a stranger in a strange place, I was very lonely, indeed; but the following little verse, which I repeated again and again, cheered me very much:—

"Perhaps this feeble frame of mine
    Shall soon in sickness lie,
But, trusting in the precious blood,
    How peacefully I'll die!"

In the morning I telegraphed to Ireland for Mr. Kingston, who arrived the next day and remained with me for a few weeks, when I was able to return home. I will never forget his kindness: he was so attentive to me all through my illness.

I had seasons of great nervous prostration, and Satan took advantage of my weakness, and many were the conflicts of soul that I had during the following year. He would suggest that I should never preach again, and that all my years of preaching were a blank, and that I had never been converted at all.

I was so deeply troubled that on one occasion I asked my wife if she remembered the time when I was saved, or if she thought there was any reality in my profession. I truly understood in some measure the words of Ephesians 6:12: "For we wrestle not against flesh and blood, but against principalities and powers, against the rulers of the darkness of this world, against spiritual wickedness in high places."

Mr. and Mrs. Stewart, who at that time were staying at the Spa, Ballynahinch, invited my daughter, Rachel, and myself to spend a month with them there. Although still in very poor health, I decided to go, and while in the train I felt so weak that I began to wonder if I should live until I reached my destination; but by the time I arrived at the Spa I was much better, and at the end of the month my health had greatly improved. I had a very refreshing time while here. Our company included Mr. and Mrs. Jeremiah Meneely, of Ballymena, and the happy fellowship which we had together was most blessed.

*While here I had a most remarkable dream. I dreamed I saw Christ on the Cross. I cannot describe His appearance, He was so beautiful and heavenly. I heard Him speak to the thief and say, "Today shalt thou be with me in Paradise," and as He uttered these words, the thief suddenly changed into His image. The scene was so glorious that I commenced to clap my hands, and awoke in the act of doing so. What a sight it will be to see the King in His beauty, and to be changed into His own glorious likeness!

Mr. and Mrs. White, of Tandragee, kindly invited me to their house for an indefinite period in the hope that my health would continue to improve. I went there from the Spa but, although they showed me great kindness, I progressed very slowly, and in a short time was obliged to return home.

After I had been six months at home, my health having somewhat improved, I had a strong desire to preach the Gospel again. As I was not yet able to walk far, I hired a house convenient to where I lived, and held some meetings there. I thanked God that I once more had the privilege of preaching Christ to the lost and perishing.

*It is interesting to note that, about thirty-two years after having this dream, David Rea passed peacefully away to be for ever with the Lord, from this very place, the Spa.

CLANROOT, PORTADOWN, 1885

A pressing invitation was given me to take up Gospel work in this place, which is about four miles from where I resided. Although still unable to undergo much exertion, I did not hesitate to comply with the request, as I believed the Lord desired me to continue to preach the Word.

At this time I had a dream which served to strengthen my conviction that I should go to Clanroot. I dreamed that I was preaching to a large crowd of men. All, except one, appeared to be angry with me, and he, taking me by the arm, led me to the foot of an embankment, where there was a well of water. I dropped my purse, in which there were seven shillings and sixpence, and it fell into the water. While I was looking for it I picked up a gentleman's pocket-book, which on opening I found to be well-nigh filled with mud, but on examining it more closely I saw that it contained several small pieces of gold, each shaped like a heart. While I was extracting these precious little golden pieces I awoke.

I interpreted my dream as a token that the Lord had at Clanroot a number of precious gems which He was going to extract from the rubbish-heap there, and that I was to be the instrument in His hands for that purpose.

I went, and at my first meeting the place was crowded with people, and the presence and power of God were realised in a great measure. I continued here for several months, the attendance so increasing that frequently large numbers were unable to gain admission to the hall.

I was still very weak in body, and often had to rest when on the platform. Sometimes I was so unable to stand while preaching that it was with difficulty I kept from falling. Neverthelesss, the Lord manifested His power in the saving of many souls.

I taught the converts to gather together on the first day of the week, to remember the Lord in the breaking of bread. On the first occasion on which we met fifty sat around the table, and we had a happy time together at that meeting. How blessed it is to thus assemble, owning no name but Jesus!

Eventually I was unable through ill-health to continue any longer, but the Lord supplied the need of the district and sent over from Glasgow our brother Francis Logg, who took up the work of preaching the Gospel and the ministry of the Word to the saints.

Mr. James Stewart, of Lisburn, on hearing of my illness, kindly rented a house for a month for myself and family at the Spa, Ballynahinch. I had improved so much during my previous visit there that he thought it was the best place for me to go.

We went, and I was again greatly benefited in health by the change; and, after leaving that place, I took a house in the country, a short distance from Portadown, my health continuing to improve.

There were a number of farm office-houses attached to the residence, and in them I made a meeting-place which held more than three hundred people. I commenced Gospel meetings, and conferences of Christians were occasionally held there.

I made a baptistry, which was also a great

convenience, and more than one hundred Believers were baptised in this place.

COUNTY ARMAGH, 1886

I again united with Mr. Logg in tent-work, and we continued for the season in County Armagh, during which time the Lord put forth His power in the salvation of souls in almost every meeting we held.

We often saw strong young men weeping bitterly and trembling from head to foot as we brought the realities of Eternity before them. Numbers of such persons accepted Christ as their Saviour and witnessed boldly for Him in the district. It was inspiring to see their readiness to follow the Lord in baptism and in gathering together in His Name.

A young woman was so awakened at our meetings that for several days she was unable to attend to her work. Her brother talked to her about her soul at her home and asked her to read the 27th chapter of Matthew, while he went into another room to pray that the Lord would reveal Himself to her. When he returned a short time afterwards he found her rejoicing and praising God for having saved her. "How did it happen?" enquired he. She replied, "It was when I came to the 42nd verse of the chapter, 'He saved others: Himself He cannot save.' The Holy Spirit revealed to me that He took the judgment due to me and bore my sins 'in His own body on the tree'" (1 Peter 2:24).

At the end of the tent season the interest was so great and so many were anxious about their souls that we hired a barn for further meetings, and many more were saved in this place.

On one occasion a widow came to the meeting, and as she was about to enter she paused on the stairs that led to the barn, and said to herself, "Here goes a sinner to hear what God has got to say to her."

Truly God did speak to her. Night after night she came, and deeper and deeper the Sword of the Spirit entered her heart, revealing to her the awful judgment that awaits the rejector of Christ.

She was so miserable that to work or sleep was impossible, and one night about twelve o'clock her cries for mercy so frightened her children that they pleaded with her to be calm. "How can I be calm, children?" she said, "when I am on the brink of Hell and your father is in Heaven?"

About an hour later the light of the glorious Gospel shone in upon her troubled soul, and she found peace through trusting in Christ. So great was her joy that she immediately went out and aroused some of the Christians in the neighbourhood, and together they rejoiced and praised the Lord for several hours.

Chapter 14

GLASGOW AND DUNDEE (SECOND VISIT)

1887

We visited Glasgow, Dundee, and several other places, preaching the Word, and had many open doors and pressing invitations while in Scotland.

On our last Lord's Day in Dundee we preached five times: first at nine o'clock in the morning to a congregation of about six hundred "outcasts of society," who assembled for the Sunday morning free breakfast. The sight of so many human wrecks on the ocean of life, all loved of God, brought the tears to my eyes.

Our audience at the afternoon service was a most interesting one. It consisted of about five hundred members of the "Young Men's Bible Class."

In this meeting I met a young man who was soon going to China as a missionary, and he told me that he had been brought to Christ in a tent-meeting which I had held ten years previously.

ACTON, 1887

This is a small village in the County Armagh, about two miles from Poyntzpass.

On our return from Scotland we pitched our tent here. The attendance was very small, the people seemingly indifferent to the Gospel; and we saw very little manifestations of blessing.

I had, however, great cause for rejoicing in my own family at this time, as the Lord saved three of my daughters.

Some Christians, friends from Glasgow, were spending their holidays at my home. I had been deeply concerned about the conversion of my children; and, although I had frequently spoken to them about their souls, and earnestly prayed that the Lord would save them, yet, when the answer came, I was so overjoyed that I could scarcely believe it.

My eldest daughter, Marianne, was the first to trust Christ. When I returned from the tent she told me that she had been saved that afternoon, and we praised the Lord together until about eleven o'clock.

About one o'clock on the same night I was awakened by my second and third daughters, Rachel and Henrietta, coming into my bedroom to tell me that they had both been saved.

My joy that night was unspeakable. I could do nothing but praise and thank God for His mercies. How like our good and gracious Lord it is thus to surprise us with His blessings!

Mrs. Logg, the sister-in-law of my fellow-labourer, was used of God in leading my girls to the Saviour.

BALLYKEEL, 1887

We next pitched our tent in Ballykeel, but very few attended our meetings, and when we had been about a week here a severe storm blew our tent down. We did not re-erect it in this place. We had the joy, however, before we left of seeing our landlady brought to Christ. We had believed her to be most indifferent to the "things of God," and were very much surprised when she awoke us one morning about four o'clock, and, clapping her hands, told us that she had just been saved.

She had been in such distress of soul that she had not gone to bed that night, and her conversion was very real.

BESSBROOK, 1887 (SECOND VISIT)

We went from Ballykeel to Bessbrook, where we spent two months. We had a time of much blessing, but encountered great opposition from the day we pitched our tent until we left.

Despite the fact that we had a watchman, we were obliged to obtain the assistance of the police, who had to come from a town two miles distant, there being no force in Bessbrook.

Several attempts were made by our opponents to haul the tent down upon us while the meetings were going on, and it was severely cut by stones which were thrown upon it. Frequently some of these came through the canvas, to the discomfiture of our audience inside. On one occasion they burned it badly with vitriol.

We were scoffed at while going to and from the tent, and jeered at when walking in the streets of the town. Notwithstanding all this, the Lord manifested His power mightily, and many souls were saved.

We baptized ten Believers on a Saturday afternoon in a river in the vicinity. A large crowd of people assembled to witness the baptism, and on the same evening they kindled bonfires throughout the neighbourhood in derision and mockery.

They also erected a platform close to our tent, and advertised by posters, handbills, and public announcements that an opposition meeting was to be held there on the following day (Sunday), to commence at the same hour as that appointed for our service. We held a special prayer-meeting that night, and felt the Lord's presence very near.

Great excitement prevailed in the town during the next day, and from early in the afternoon the people flocked in to hear the "opposition speaker." When we arrived at the field in which our tent was pitched our opponent was addressing from the newly-erected platform an audience of about three thousand, and as we came forward he paused in his address, and scornfully pointed us out to his hearers. We passed into the tent, but only a few had come to our meeting, and some of their faces bore a most terror-stricken appearance. Indeed they required great courage to have come into the tent at all.

We conducted our service amid great confusion, but in this instance the Lord was swift to defend His Truth, as the poor scorner, who had pointed us out to his audience with such derision, lost his reason before he left the platform and became a maniac.

Next day he was found wandering through the streets of Dublin raving mad, two days later, in a frenzy of insanity, he threw himself out of a window, and shortly afterwards was confined in a lunatic asylum.

Several others who took prominent parts in the opposition had also solemn visitations from the Lord. "It is a fearful thing to fall into the hands of the living God."

We visited the people at their houses, and spoke with them about their souls. On one occasion Mr. Logg handed a woman a tract, and tried to speak to her about Eternity, but she retorted, with an air of bravado, that she was going to Hell, and would deliver any message which he wished to send there. She died suddenly a few weeks afterwards, without having shown any evidence of repentance. "He, that being often reproved hardeneth his neck, shall suddenly be destroyed, and that without remedy."

We gathered together the converts on the first day of the week, to remember the Lord in the "breaking of bread." We had the assistance and co-operation of Mr. James Stewart here, who was very helpful in ministering the Word to the saints and establishing them in the Truth.

Bessbrook has a population of 3,400 people, is without a public-house, pawnship, or police barracks, and is called the "Model Village of Ireland."

KILMORE, 1887-1888, COUNTY ARMAGH

This is a district about three miles from Lurgan. I visited Mr. Archibald Bell, who exclaimed immediately I entered his house, "Well, I'm glad to see you! I have been asking the Lord to send you here." I enquired what he wanted with me, and he replied that he had hired a barn at Kilmore for the preaching of the Gospel, and wanted me to assist him with the work there. I readily agreed to accompany him, as the first meeting was to be held that night.

Although the evening was very cold and the snow lay thick upon the ground, when we arrived at the place we found about forty people sitting in the cold barn. I preached first, and took for my subject "the barren fig-tree." The Lord gave me liberty in proclaiming the Gospel, and ere I had finished speaking the tears were running down the cheeks of many of my audience.

Mr. Bell closed the meeting, and as we were going out a young woman knelt down near the door and asked us to pray the Lord to save her soul. We did so, but she did not then find peace.

We went away, but when about two hundred yards from the barn a young woman came running out of a house, and shouted to us, "Stop, please, stop. Come in here." We went in, and I shall never forget the sight which met our eyes. There on the floor of that house knelt three grown-up women and a young girl, with arms upraised, all pleading to God to save them.

We knelt down beside them, and asked God to reveal Christ to these anxious souls, and in a few minutes one of them, the mother of the girl, rose and went out praising God for having saved her.

By this time a number of people had gathered around the door outside, and when we left they came in and remained until after midnight.

When we returned to the meeting on the following evening we were introduced to seven women and a young man who had passed from "death unto life" in the house into which we had been called on the previous night.

This was the commencement of a great work of God in this district. The Believers afterwards met together on the first day of the week to break bread, and a Sunday School was commenced the Lord also manifesting His power in the salvation of some of the children.

Mr. Bell has been greatly used of God in this district, both in the preaching of the Gospel and the ministry of the Word for the edification of the saints.

CLONES, 1888

We had been praying to the Lord for guidance as to where I should take the tent in the following summer, and Clones had been impressed upon my mind. So when the season arrived we set about securing ground in this place.

We found it difficult to obtain this, but at length were promised a portion at the entrance to the town. The day following our arrangement, however, I received a letter from the landlord, inquiring to which section of the Protestant Church we belonged.

I replied that we belonged to no particular section of the Protestant Church, but that we were connected with all who loved the Lord Jesus Christ, and preached the Gospel to all without distinction of class or creed. The next day I received another letter, stating that as we belonged to no particular section of the Protestant Church we could not have the ground.

At this time we had our tent at the Railway Station for conveyance to Clones, so we went on and secured ground about a mile outside the town.

We held our first meeting on a Lord's Day evening, but at the time appointed to commence and for some time afterwards not an individual, except ourselves, had entered the tent, although a noisy crowd of Roman Catholics had assembled outside. This was very trying to us, but before we left that evening a fair number had come in, and the Lord enabled us to preach His Word. We continued here for several weeks, and many were convicted of sin and brought to the Lord Jesus Christ.

One night about half-an-hour before the time to commence our meeting a woman came into the tent and sat down near the platform, sobbing bitterly. Suddenly she began to praise God for having saved her, and told us that she had not slept for several nights, so great was her distress about her soul. She came to our first meeting, and, although she had been a Sunday School teacher for twenty-five years, she found out that she had never been "born again." But she was convicted of sin and brought to Christ.

A young man, who had been aroused to see his need of salvation at these meetings, found peace at two o'clock in the morning, and awoke the household to tell them of the Saviour he had found.

Many individual cases of conversion at Clones

might be recorded, but it is sufficient to say that the Lord manifested His power in the awakening and saving of many sinners in this place.

Part 2

Chapter 15

The preceding chapters contain the entire matter left on record by my father, and cover the period from his conversion in 1869 until the year 1888.

When I was in conversation with him regarding his writings, he said, in a somewhat sad tone, "Tom, it is not finished yet," from which I concluded that, had he recovered, he would have completed the record of his labours in the Gospel.

It is gratifying, however, to be able to state that I have obtained from other sources a fairly accurate account of many of the most notable Gospel campaigns which he has not related. These I hope to record in their order and in as intelligent language as my feeble ability as a writer can command; and, being fully conscious of my incompetence to produce a perfect literary work, I crave the indulgence of my readers for any errors which they may discover herein.

BALLYMENA, 1892 (SECOND VISIT)

On the invitation of some friends my father went to Ballymena in September, 1892, to conduct a mission for one week; but the interest became so great that, with the exception of a few days' rest which he took in the latter end of October, he continued here for four months.

The power of God was manifested from the very first, and the attendance so increased that the

largest hall in the town, which held more than one
thousand people, was crowded nightly by men and
women eager to hear the Gospel.

So greatly were the people convicted of sin that
considerable difficulty was experienced in getting
the hall cleared before midnight; and some who had
left earlier were too much distressed to go to their
homes unsaved, and returned to the hall to cry to
God for mercy. Others sought the quietude of their
homes to cry unto the Lord for salvation, many of
whom were enabled in their own houses to rest
their souls upon the finished work of Christ.

Frequently friends and relations, parents and
children, would be seen in groups together praising
God and weeping for joy over some of their number
who had just found peace.

A few miles outside the town mid-day meetings
were held in a barn, which was often filled with
people. Such was the thirst for the Word of God
that many ceased their work, some walking seven
miles to attend these services. Hundreds were
brought to Christ during this mission, and a large
number were baptized and added to the assemblies
in the neighbourhood.

Some of the older inhabitants who had witnessed
the scenes of 1859, spoke of this work being, in
some respects, as remarkable as that great movement.

BALLYWATERMOY, GLARRYFORD, AND CLOUGH, 1893

The news of the work in Ballymena created such

an interest among the people of the surrounding districts that he decided to take a preaching tour in the neighbourhood within a circuit of six or eight miles.

He went first to Ballywatermoy, and from thence to Glarryford, which is about three miles distant, and afterwards to the village of Clough.

These places were all scenes of great blessing. Saints were revived in soul and stimulated to more energy in the service of God, and many sinners were brought to Christ.

BROUGHSHANE, 1893

After leaving Clough, my father went to Brough-shane, which is a village of about five hundred inhabitants, situated three and a half miles from Ballymena, at the entrance of the Braid Valley.

Determined efforts were made to keep him out of this village and district, and the people were in some measure influenced by the plausible argument that he had been rending family ties in other places. He endeavoured to obtain the use of the Courthouse, but, although a promise had been given that it would be available, he found at the last moment that it had been decided not to allow him to conduct his services there. Subsequently he was able to secure a room in the village, which held about one hundred people. This was almost filled the first night, and on the third evening it was so crowded that large numbers had to stand outside.

The power and presence of God were manifested, and it was with difficulty that the people could be got to disperse at the close of the service.

At the sight of so many standing outside, unable to gain admission, his sympathy was aroused; and at the end of the meeting he stood up, Bible in hand, and exclaimed that it was deplorable to see the people standing outside on a cold winter night for lack of accommodation, while large buildings in Broughshane were shut against him for the proclamation of the Gospel.

The Lord spoke through this word to those in authority, and the Courthouse was available for his meeting on the following evening. The attendance continued to increase, and on the next Lord's Day the house was packed with people an hour before the time, all eager to hear the Gospel; and by the time appointed for the service to commence hundreds were standing outside, unable to gain an entrance. So great was the throng that when my father came up to the door a policeman, with the assistance of some friends, was obliged to take hold of him and pull him into the building, almost over the heads of the people.

When the service was concluded the crowd standing outside pleaded with him to speak to them from the window. Several had walked twelve miles to this meeting, and had to return that night. He had on that occasion to stop speaking owing to the cries and lamentations of those anxious about their souls, and on the same night twenty professed to have passed from death unto life before the meeting separated.

On the second Lord's Day the people were assembling at 3.30 p.m., although the time appointed to commence the service was 7 p.m. So great was the crowd that it was considered inadvisable to open the door of the Courthouse, lest an accident should ensue through the rush to get in; but as the night was calm a platform was erected outside, from which he addressed the audience.

At the close of the meeting my father invited those who were anxious to come into the building, and for several hours a remarkable time of blessing was experienced.

A Roman Catholic young man walked eleven miles to attend this meeting, and at four o'clock the next morning, while on his way home, found peace through believing in the Lord Jesus Christ.

Mid-day meetings were held daily in several places throughout the country. These were largely attended, and the Coming Day only will reveal the extent of the blessing received through this mission at Broughshane in the early part of the year 1893.

ABERDEEN, 1894

He visited Aberdeen in January, 1894, for the purpose of conducting a Gospel campaign. A large hall in The Guestron, off Castlegate, was taken for the occasion. God commenced to work wonderfully in these meetings: hundreds of people attended nightly.

The attendance so increased that it was found necessary to obtain a larger building for the Lord's Day evening meetings and, having secured the Palace Theatre in Bridge Street, the Christians assembled in Castlegate at 7.30 p.m., and marched in large procession by way of Union Street to the Theatre, singing praises to the Lord Who had redeemed them, the local evangelical missions all joining in hearty co-operation with them. One of the hymns frequently sung was:—

> "Alas! and did my Saviour bleed,
>   And did my Sovereign die?
> Did He devote that sacred head
>   For such a worm as I?
> Oh, the blood of Jesus, the precious blood of
>   Jesus
>   Oh, the blood of Jesus, it cleanseth from all
>   sin."

It was a glorious sight — a sight to make angels rejoice — to see the thousands who accompanied the band of singers to the building on these cold, wintry nights, drawn by no other attraction save the prospect of hearing the Gospel proclaimed in its simplicity.

Although the Theatre held two thousand people, it was often almost filled before the time announced to commence; and when the procession arrived, hundreds were unable to gain admission. While the meeting was going on inside, several Christian workers preached to those who were standing around the door.

He devoted a special night for all who wished to testify as to what the grace of God had done for them, and intimated that any Christians who wished to give their testimonies, but felt too timid to speak to a large audience, should write them, and he would read them from the platform, after which they would be asked to stand up as witnesses to the written testimonies. This was done, and a large number of testimonies to the saving and keeping power of the Lord Jesus Christ were handed in and read in public, the writer afterwards standing up in confirmation of the written record.

His last day here was one long to be remembered. The large theatre was crowded to its utmost capacity, and the presence and power of God were manifested in most marked degree. During this mission, which was brought to a close on the second Lord's Day of February, 1894, scores of people professed conversion, saints were revived, and Eternity alone will reveal the work accomplished through the grace of God at this series of meetings in the "Granite City."

BARNSTAPLE (NORTH DEVON), 1894

He was invited to conduct a series of meetings in Barnstaple, in October, 1894. The Music Hall, which is the largest in the town, was obtained for the Sunday night meeting, and this was filled at each service.

Prayer-meetings were held daily in a smaller hall, and large numbers of requests for prayer and thanksgiving were sent in. These were seasons of rich blessing.

The Lord's people were much refreshed and greatly helped.

Many sinners were awakened as to their state before God, and a large number passed from "death unto life" through accepting the Lord Jesus Christ as their Saviour.

Our brother, Mr. W. H. Stranger, in describing this work in a religious journal under date of November 1st, 1894, concludes by saying, "We thank God for our brother's visit."

GALWAY (FIRST VISIT), 1895

He was invited by a Christian lady to conduct a mission in the town of Galway. He went in the autumn of 1895, and commenced in a hall which had been procured for the occasion.

About this time the late Mr. James Buchanan of Cork, with several other fellow-labourers, had been endeavouring to conduct open-air services in this town. On the Sunday previous to his coming, these friends had been so severely maltreated, although guarded by the police, that they had been obliged to take refuge in the hall in which it had been arranged that he should conduct his services, and so badly had they been abused that when he arrived a week later blood stains were still discernible within the precincts of the building.

The authorities, having heard that he intended holding open-air services, warned him against doing so, stating that they could not possibly protect him. He replied that he could hold his meeting without their protection; and when they saw that he was determined to carry out his resolve, they offered to send him a guard of police; but he told them that he did not require their assistance, and that his confidence was in God, Whom he trusted to preserve him from injury.

Accordingly, at the time arranged for his open-air service, he took his stand in Eyre Square, and was soon surrounded by hundreds of the inhabitants of this almost entirely Roman Catholic town.

He requested them to give him a hearing, saying he would endeavour to speak as loudly as possible, and for about half-an-hour he preached the Gospel in its simplicity.

On looking down the street he perceived a large crowd coming towards him, and for the moment he was slightly disconcerted; but as it drew nearer he saw that it was a funeral procession, the coffin being drawn in a farm cart.

He ceased speaking until it had passed, and then continued his address for a further half-hour, at the conclusion of which he said: "Now, boys, did you all hear me?" and many replied, "Yes, sir." Before leaving he went amongst them, and shook hands with a number of them, bidding them "Good-bye," and not one attempted to molest him or spoke a disparaging word of him.

Chapter 16

GLASGOW, 1895 and 1896

He and Mr. Alexander Marshall commenced in a theatre in the East End of the City, but after a few weeks my father went to the West End, where a hall had been taken. Here he began daily prayer-meetings, and many Christians united with him for several weeks, praying that God would bless the services held at night. God heard their prayers and answered beyond all expectations.

Soon the numbers so increased that on week-nights the hall was well filled, and on Sundays it was packed to overflowing. The Spirit began to move upon the hearts of hardened sinners, and from many the cry went up, "What must I do to be saved?"

The attendance was so great that a larger hall was necessary, and he succeeded in securing the "Olympic," which was close at hand and capable of holding ten thousand people. Strange to say, two Christian women had for the previous eighteen months been earnestly praying that God would open this very place for the Gospel.

It came as a great surprise to all that the "Olympic" had been taken. Long before the time arranged for the first meeting crowds were standing outside waiting for admission, and when the doors were thrown open the rush to get in almost caused a panic.

The numbers increased nightly until more than ten thousand, composed of almost all creeds and classes of society, were to be seen standing jammed together in this huge building listening to the Gospel. The meeting usually continued for about two hours, and, as someone remarked when entering, "What a wonderful sight, and nothing but the Gospel!"

On the last Friday night of the meetings a man and his wife were seated in different parts of the hall. They both trusted Christ and were saved, and were baptized at the baptismal service at the close of the meeting.

On the following Sunday they both met with an assembly of Christians to remember the Lord in the breaking of bread, and several years afterwards Mr. J. B. Kingston heard that they were going on steadily, "adorning the doctrine of Christ."

Over one hundred professed faith in Christ during this mission, and my father baptised sixty-two Believers, four Roman Catholics being among them.

CHAPEL FIELDS, BELFAST, 1897

This place is situated about two hundred yards from the new City Hall, and is the rendezvous of thousands of young people who assemble at the holiday seasons to amuse themselves with the various sports and entertainments introduced by what are known as the "Show-people." These pastimes provide amusement in the form of hobby-horses, swing-boats, shooting galleries, etc.

The grounds are now extensively built upon and almost surrounded by great warehouses, which largely conceal them from the view of the passers-by, but at the time they were within the view of anyone going through Ormeau Avenue. My father often said that his heart ached at the sight of so many giddy young men and women being lured on their downward path of destruction by these frivolities.

With that determination and aggressiveness which always characterised him in his service for God, he decided, when opportunity offered, to plant the standard of the Cross and unfurl the banner of salvation upon the very ground which had for so many years been allotted to the wandering showmen, whose enchantments fascinated the frolicsome pleasure-seekers, congregating in such large numbers at Christmas, Easter, and July.

Hence his great desire to obtain a large circus-shaped tent, capable of holding two or three thousand people, and to place in it four or five benches, diverging backwards in an upward direction, with an elevation of about eighteen inches from each other, and extending on either side to the platform, thus forming a sort of circular gallery right round the tent, the centre to be provided with movable seats. With such a construction he would be able to speak to a large audience with some degree of ease.

Thus he became his own architect, and, having obtained the large tent, which was made and pitched by Messrs. R. Christy and Co., of Corporation Street, Belfast, he secured the services of skilled workmen to carry out his designs regarding the seating accommodation. Accordingly on the 22nd day of June, 1897, Mr. Henry G. Gibson, on entering the tent about two hours after its erection in the Chapel Fields, found my father superintending the work of providing seats for his large and famous canvas tent.

He encouraged him in the undertaking, and offered to do any little service that he could in connection with the work; and he states that he was well rewarded for any service rendered by the hearty "Thank you" and look of delight, as Mr. Rea said, "I am glad to see the face of any sympathising Christian."

Despite the ironical remarks of some of his incredulous friends, who were doubtful as to the wisdom of erecting so huge a structure in such a place as the Chapel Fields, he persevered in the work, and had seating accommodation completed for two thousand people at five o'clock in the afternoon of the following Saturday, and at seven o'clock on the same evening a prayer-meeting was held inside the newly-erected tent, about twenty Christians attending. The power of God was felt in this meeting, and the unanimous opinion was that as he had gone in for great things the Lord was going to honour his faith and, without a doubt, He did so.

The following is a verbatim copy of the first newspaper announcement in relation to his work in the Chapel Fields, which appeared in the Saturday issue of the *Evening Telegraph* of the 26th June, 1897:—

THE LARGE NEW CIRCULAR TENT

Seating over 2,000 is now pitched on the Show Grounds. Entrance by Linenhall Street.

MEETINGS COMMENCING (D.V.)

On SUNDAY EVENING, JUNE 27th, at Eight o'clock

WEEK-NIGHTS at the same hour.

Doors open at 7.30.

PREACHER — MR. DAVID REA

THE PRAYERS AND SYMPATHY OF ALL CHRISTIANS are earnestly asked for a Special Outpouring of the Spirit of God upon this work, that the Name of the Lord Jesus Christ only may be glorified in the Salvation of many souls.

SPECIAL PRAYER MEETINGS:

SATURDAY, June 26th, at 7 p.m.
SUNDAY, June 27th, at 9 a.m.

A large number attended the nine o'clock Sunday morning prayer-meeting, and great liberty was felt in their approaches to God by those who led in prayer in this meeting. But what a spectacle was presented to the view at the next meeting, which was held at eight o'clock on that evening!

Every seat in this enormous tent was occupied, and around the platform, in the aisles, and at the door hundreds of people stood, all apparently eager to hear the Gospel.

A friend who was present that night states that the view from the platform was awe-inspiring. Look to the right, look to the left, or gaze in front of you—nothing was to be seen but a vast sea of faces, while all listened intently to every word spoken by the preacher.

The power of God was greatly manifested, and at the close of the service many professed to have trusted Christ.

The early prayer meetings on Sunday mornings were well attended. Several hundreds remained behind, at the night services, for the after-meetings, which often lasted until eleven o'clock, and souls were saved almost every night.

Many young women employed in the warehouses and factories in the vicinity were converted, and a dinner-hour service was held in the tent for the convenience of these girls. It was not unusual to see five or six hundred at these meal-hour meetings, as many preferred attending them to going home for dinner.

A number were led to Christ in their places of business through the testimony of fellow-employees who had been saved at the tent.

Some thought it inadvisable to hold a Gospel service on the twelfth of July, their opinion being that the attendance would be very small, as this was a day of great excitement in Belfast, and the people would probably be too much occupied with celebrating the "Twelfth of July Demonstration" to attend the meeting.

He decided, however, to hold his service at the usual time, and, although the meeting was somewhat smaller than usual, the presence and power of God were felt in a most remarkable degree. Eleven professed to have received Christ that night, and some of these afterwards became active Christian workers and great soul-winners.

On a Saturday afternoon, in the month of August, Mrs. W.H. M'Laughlin provided a tea in the tent for the converts and their friends, and more than one thousand partook of this repast.

The Duke and Duchess of York paid a Royal visit to Belfast on Wednesday, 8th September, 1897. The day was a general holiday; the City was the scene of much excitement, and was gaily decorated for their reception. My father, with his usual forethought, saw what a splendid opportunity this would afford to witness for Christ, and arranged that the Christians should march in procession on that day, holding aloft banners containing appropriate Gospel texts.

The streets of the City were lined with tens of thousands of people, who had gathered from all parts of the province to welcome the Duke and his Consort, and just as the Royal procession passed at the junction of Ann Street and Victoria Street, the band of over five hundred Christians stepped in at the rear, with banners bearing Scripture texts and announcements of the meetings. Thousands followed them in their march through Victoria Street,

High Street, Castle Place, Donegall Place, and
Bedford Street, singing as they went that beautiful
hymn:—

> "All hail the power of Jesu's name;
>   Let angels prostrate fall;
> Bring forth the royal diadem,
>   And crown Him Lord of all.
>
> Let high-born seraphs tune the lyre,
>   And as they tune it, fall
> Before His face who formed their choir,
>   And crown Him Lord of all.
>
> Ye souls, redeemed of Adam's race,
>   Ye ransomed from the fall;
> Hail Him who saved you by His grace,
>   And crown Him Lord of all.
>
> Ye saints whose love can ne'er forget
>   The wormwood and the gall,
> Go spread your trophies at His feet,
>   And crown Him Lord of all.
>
> O soon with yonder sacred throng
>   We at His feet shall fall,
> Join in the everlasting song,
>   And crown Him Lord of all."

A prayer-meeting, which was well attended, was
then held in the tent, and helpful addresses were
delivered to Christians.

The interest was so great and the power of God

so manifest that at the end of October it was decided that the meetings should be continued through the winter. A number of gas stoves were procured and placed in the tent, and Mr. W. H. McLauglin, at great cost, provided a waterproof covering for the roof.

My father intended continuing to the beginning of the spring, but in December his ground landlord sent him a notice to the effect that the "Show-people" required the ground at Christmas, and that he would be obliged to leave before that time.

It was with much regret that he took the tent down about the 18th of the month, after perhaps one of the most prolonged missions that has ever been held under canvas. During the six months hundreds of souls were brought to Christ, and many state that this was the greatest work of God ever conducted in Belfast.

He was greatly assisted in the work by the late Mr. James Stewart, of Lisburn, who came three nights in each week, and by Mr. W. H. McLaughlin, who was a great help in both the evening and mid-day meetings. The late Lord Carrick also attended frequently, and several other notable Christian workers.

Chapter 17

DUBLIN (FIRST VISIT), 1898

In the month of May, 1898, he took his large tent to Dublin, and pitched it on a vacant piece of ground in Tara Street, a district surrounded by hundreds of poor Roman Catholics.

He held two meetings daily—a prayer-meeting at mid-day, and a Gospel service in the evening. The week-night meetings were usually well attended, and on Sundays the tent was crowded, about one-third of the audience being Roman Catholics. Many were brought to Christ and witnessed brightly for the Lord. It was a glorious sight to see so many converted Roman Catholics standing up in the testimony meetings, which were held every Friday, and witnessing to the saving and keeping power of the Lord Jesus Christ, stating that they had trusted Jesus, and had found full satisfaction in Him, and no longer feared the priests. On one occasion in one of these meetings a father, son, and daughter, all of whom had been saved in the tent, stood up together and testified as to what the Lord had done for them.

The last tent-meeting of that season, which was held on Sunday, the 16th of October, was one long to be remembered. The place was packed to overflowing, and many souls were saved.

The tent was taken down on the following day, and my father united with Mr. Brunton, who was conducting services in Merrion Hall. The power of

God was also manifested in these meetings, and many sinners were saved.

On his last Sunday night the hall was crowded at the seven o'clock service and, as many were standing outside unable to gain admission, he decided to hold a second service from 8.15 to 9.30.

At this meeting the hall was again crowded. Additional seats had to be obtained from the Lower Hall, and the people were standing in the aisles, around the door, and on the stairs. One who was present states: "It was a magnificent sight to see dear old Merrion Hall, with its two circular galleries and capacious area, packed to its utmost limits, as Mr. Rea proclaimed from the platform the glorious truth of a free and full salvation through faith in the precious blood of the Lord Jesus Christ."

The power of God was upon the meeting, and many passed from "death unto life." Some of the older Christians said that they had not seen anything like the work here since the "Revival of 1859."

The following incidents, which occurred while he was in Dublin, are worth relating: On one occasion, when preaching, he was wearing a pair of detachable cuffs, which frequently came down over his hands. This so worried him that he pulled them off, and flinging them behind him said, in a low voice, "Go long, ye hypocrites." On another occasion he was wearing a new pair of elastic-sided boots, which creaked noisily as he moved about the platform. This annoyed him so much that, in his usual impulsive manner, he ceased speaking and, stooping down drew off the boots, flung them to one side, and then continued his address as though nothing unusual had occurred.

LIVERPOOL, 1899

Mr. James Johnston, of Liscard, Chester, was a staunch friend of my father's, and visited him in Dublin in 1898. He was so interested in his work there that before he left he invited him to bring his tent to Liverpool in the following summer.

At that time the erection of Crete Hall was almost completed, and he was invited to attend the opening service. He went, and while there he conducted a week's special meetings, which were well attended, some souls being saved.

He was again besought to take up tent-work in Liverpool, and before he left it was arranged that he should dispatch the tent from Dublin to be stored in Liverpool until the following summer, when it could be pitched in that place.

Accordingly in the summer of 1899 he set about having the tent pitched in Fairclough Lane, Liverpool, a very poor and needy district, whose population was mainly composed of Jews and Roman Catholics, living without God.

At this time the tent was capable of holding two thousand people, but for some time previous to that summer he had contemplated enlarging it, so that it might hold another thousand (i.e., three thousand in all). After much careful consideration and prayer for guidance, this he proceeded to do. The difficulties of the project were overwhelming and

almost insurmountable, but he never wavered from
his purpose, trusting in God to supply all his needs.
Tons of earth had to be removed from the site
chosen, and the cost of the amount of extra timber
for props, staves, and seats, and of the canvas for
covering of such a large circumference, formed a
heavy financial cloud which loomed darkly on the
horizon.

Then the Town Building Surveyor appeared on
the scene, and demanded that certain strengths of
timber should be put into the tent for safety. At this
juncture some of the Christians thought it would
be better to leave matters as they were, and have
the tent fixed without enlargement, but my father's
vigorous personality and enthusiasm completely
overruled their objections.

The Christians, with one accord, met together
nightly and on Saturday afternoons at Fairclough
Lane, and with spade, pick, and wheelbarrow,
commenced the long and arduous task of levelling
the site. This task occupied about five weeks, and
many Christians can still look back upon it as a
labour indeed in the Master's service.

The site cleared, and the tent erected, my father
came over from Belfast (where he had been on a
flying visit) to inspect it. Upon entering it for the
first time, after its erection in Fairclough Lane, he
walked to the furthermost seat at the back, sat
down and, in a voice full of thankfulness, exclaimed,
"Thank God! It's just lovely."

The Gospel work commenced, and went on
without a break for four months, many souls being
saved nightly, and not a few being added to the

assemblies in Liverpool through this good work. Many young men and women of Christian parentage were brought to the Lord during this mission, and some of them later laboured for God in Central Asia and elsewhere.

Many interesting cases of conversion occurred here, one of which was that of a young man and his wife who had been separated for several years. Both attended the meetings, neither knowing that the other was present, were convicted of sin, and saved. Some time afterwards they met face to face in the tent, and not till then did each learn of the other's conversion; they did not, in fact, know until then that they had been in the same city. Their mutual joy at the good news was inexpressible, and from that time they were re-united. My father afterwards visited their home, and its appearance bore eloquent testimony to the reality of the profession of these two dear souls.

DUBLIN (SECOND VISIT), 1900

He paid a second visit to Dublin with his huge tent in the summer of 1900, where the Lord again blessed his efforts in the saving of many precious souls.

After leaving Dublin he returned to Belfast, where Mr. W. H. McLaughlin and he commenced meetings in Apsley Street Hall on Lord's Day, the 4th of November, of the same year, and continued there for several weeks.

They also held meetings at 8.15 p.m. in the Ulster

Hall, Belfast, for four successive Sunday nights, beginning on the 25th of November. At both of these places the attendance was large and many professed conversion.

Chapter 18

CHAPEL FIELDS, BELFAST, 1902

He again pitched in the Chapel Fields in the summer of 1902. This was also a time of great blessing, many souls being saved, and the work went on until the middle of November.

On Lord's Day, the 5th of October, the late Mr. J. R. Caldwell, of Glasgow, gave an address to Christians in the tent at four o'clock in the afternoon, the audience numbering almost two thousand.

He also delivered two further addresses to Believers on the Tuesday and Thursday following. The saints were much helped by the ministry of our esteemed brother, and many treasured fond recollections of these meetings.

After taking his tent down he commenced on Sunday, the 23rd of November, a series of Gospel meetings in Matchett Street Hall, Belfast, and continued for three weeks. The meetings were well attended, and the saints were greatly refreshed.

CHAPEL FIELDS, 1903

He returned here again in the month of August, 1903, and pitched the tent on its usual site.

The Christians assembled at 10 a.m. and at 4 p.m. each Sunday to pray for the Lord's blessing upon the meetings.

He resumed his mid-day services, and these were largely attended by the warehouse workers, many of whom were brought to the Lord.

A testimony meeting was held every Friday night, several brethren relating how they had been saved, and afterwards written testimonies of both brethren and sisters were read from the platform. These were very interesting meetings, and the attendance was usually very large. Many souls were saved, and the Christians were greatly helped through this mission.

TEMPLEMORE AVENUE, BELFAST, 1904

This year he decided to pitch his tent in another part of the city, and having secured ground in an open space in the lower end of Templemore Avenue, he erected it on this site.

He held his first meeting at 4 o'clock on Sunday, the 10th of July; the following opening announcement appeared in the *Belfast Evening Telegraph* on Saturday, the 9th July, 1904:—

"MR. D. REA'S
LARGE TENT, TEMPLEMORE AVENUE,
MOUNTPOTTINGER,
MEETINGS on Sunday next,
July the 10th, at 4 o'clock and 8.15 p.m.
Week-nights at 8 o'clock.

Great interest was manifested in this place from the commencement of the meetings. At the opening Sunday evening service the tent was crowded.

A most hallowed time was experienced at the fellowship Conference on the 13th July. The ministry was helpful to even the youngest believer, and was largely confined to the exhorting of Christians to live more devoted lives for the Lord, and to seek to win souls for Him. There is still a great need for such teaching in these days. If Christians only realised their responsibility towards God and man, they would show more concern for the welfare of fellow-travellers to Eternity, and would have more compassion for poor deluded sinners, rushing down the stream of time with awful rapidity to an everlasting Hell.

Many were saved in these meetings during that summer. The Christians in most of the churches in the vicinity were greatly revived, and a work for God began in the district.

Not since the great work in the Chapel Fields, in 1897, had such large numbers been brought to Christ through his tent-missions as were in Templemore Avenue, in 1904.

TEMPLEMORE AVENUE, BELFAST, 1905

He again pitched his tent in Templemore Avenue in 1905. His first meeting, which was devoted to the ministry of the Word to Christians, was held at 4 p.m. on Sunday, 9th July, and a Gospel meeting was held at 8.15 p.m. of the same day.

In his opening newspaper announcement of Saturday, the 8th of July, he invited all Christians who had an interest in the furtherance of the

Gospel and the salvation of souls, to unite with him
in earnest prayer for the blessing of God upon this
work. The Lord truly heard and answered their
prayers, and this also was a season of great blessing,
many souls being brought to know Christ as their
Saviour.

Open-air services were conducted in connection
with the tent work, and bands of Christians
marched through the streets in the district singing
hymns, and delivering short Gospel addresses to
the people around.

He was again this year greatly helped by Mr. A
Jardine, who united with him in the work.

He was desirous of continuing the meetings in
this locality throughout the winter, and with that
object in view secured ground in a more sheltered
place, near Mountpottinger Corner. He had it
sheeted around with wood, to which he attached
the canvas, and had the interior most comfortably
heated with gas stoves, but had only been here a
short time, when by some mishap or deliberate act
the tent was set on fire, and although not entirely
burned, it was badly damaged.

He was advised to claim compensation for
malicious burning, but he resolutely declined to
pursue such a course.

He continued the meetings for a few weeks in the
Y.M.C.A. Hall at Mountpottinger, but kept the tent
on the ground where the fire had taken place.

One Saturday afternoon he received a telephone
message from the police, who stated that a man was
carting away some of the material of the tent, and
enquired if this person had his authority to do so.

He replied that no one had any authority to remove it, and on hearing this the police arrested the man, who was in due course brought before the magistrates; but my father so pleaded for him, that although he was found guilty he was discharged with a caution. This gave my father an opportunity of preaching the Gospel in the Court House, and he pointed out in his defence of the culprit, that as he himself had been forgiven so many sins, he would not like to see this man punished.

Chapter 19

APSLEY STREET HALL, BELFAST, 1906

The Christians here had been greatly exercised as to putting forth a special effort in the work of the Gospel. Through removals and other causes the Assembly had somewhat decreased in numbers, and the brethren did what should always be done under such circumstances, namely — cry to God for blessing, and with heart and soul go in for the preaching of the Gospel which is the power of God unto Salvation.

One Lord's Day morning, early in the month of January, 1906, he came to Apsley Street Hall to the breaking of bread meeting, and was invited to take the service at seven o'clock that evening. He did so, and before leaving the platform, without consulting anyone, intimated that he would continue the meetings during the week. Although the Christians had made no arrangements for holding special services at that time, they heartily fell in with his announcement, and co-operated with him in what was the commencement of the greatest work for God that ever was carried on in connection with this Assembly.

From the very beginning of these services the Lord manifested His presence in great power. Souls were saved almost every night, and sometimes it was with difficulty that the congregation was dispersed, so anxious were many of them to learn

more about the way of salvation. Frequently he had
to hurry off to catch the last tram for his home,
while some of the Christian workers remained to
speak to those who were desirous of being saved.

The attendance increased nightly until every seat
in the hall was occupied at the week-night services,
and on Sunday evening it was crowded to overflowing, many being obliged to stand; although
additional seats were procured for the aisles.

On one occasion, after the meetings had been
continued for about five weeks, he said, while
announcing his next week's services, that he did not
know how long the meetings would be continued,
no one had asked him to commence, and no one had
told him to stop, and that he hoped to go on until the
work was done.

Thus night after night for fifteen weeks he went
on in this hall, over fifty having professed
conversion, thirty of whom he baptized. Most of
these were received into fellowship in the Assembly.
The saints were greatly revived, and many who had
been somewhat indifferent to the propagation of
the Gospel became active workers.

Consequently what was a Assembly small in
numbers, and apparently in great weakness when
he visited it early in January, was through the Grace
of God at the following Easter a large and
flourishing Assembly.

The tent season was now coming on, but as a
large portion of his old tent had been burned, it was
necessary that he should have it repaired, and the
Apsley Street Christians set about obtaining the
requisite funds for this purpose.

The late Mr. Samuel Cunningham, who was an
active worker in connection with all his services in
Apsley Street Hall, took the lead in this matter, and
with that energy and Christian sympathy that was
characteristic of him, entered with a willing mind
into the task of quickly procuring sufficient means
to discharge the tent makers' account, with the
result that, although the costs amounted to almost
two hundred pounds, it was obtained before the
end of the month of July of that year.

CHAPEL FIELDS, 1906

Having now got his tent renovated, he pitched it
again in the Chapel Fields, the first service being
held at four o'clock in the afternoon of Lord's Day,
the 12th August, 1906, the evening meetings
commencing at the usual time, namely 8.15 p.m. on
Sundays, and week nights at eight o'clock.

The recent revival in Apsley Street Assembly
added greatly to the interest of the tent work that
year. He frequently conducted the Sunday evening
7 o'clock service in this Hall, after which the
Christians marched in procession to the Chapel
Fields, singing hymns as they went. Occasionally
there were other churches or assemblies who
proceeded thus, and sometimes three bands of
singers were to be seen coming from different
directions to these Sunday night meetings.

His addresses at four o'clock on Lord's Days were
mostly to Christians, and were very helpful to the
new converts.

When dealing in those meetings with fundamental

doctrines, and distinct Scriptural commands, he spoke with no uncertain sound, and often with very forcible language. Nevertheless he manifested such sincerity that although his audiences were largely composed of Christians of almost all denominations, he commanded their utmost esteem.

He was occasionally assisted in these services by Mr. Charles Lepper, Mr. W.H. M'Laughlin, and on two occasions Mr. John Ritchie, Senior, of Kilmarnock, gave helpful addresses.

Throughout this season the meetings were well attended. The saints were greatly refreshed, and many sinners were convicted of sin, and converted to God.

CHAPEL FIELDS, 1907

During the winter of 1906 and 1907 he conducted Sunday night services in the different halls throughout the City of Belfast, but mostly in Apsley Street Assembly Room, where such blessing had been manifested in the early part of the former year.

As the tent season came round he again chose his old site in the Chapel Fields, and at four o'clock in the afternoon of Sunday, 28th July, 1907, he held his first meeting which was convened for Christians. The attendance was large and the ministry very helpful. The Gospel meeting at 8.15 on the same evening was also well attended, and the Christians present felt delighted indeed to be once more under the old canvas.

The week-night services were conducted as usual at eight o'clock, but half an hour before that time, he was always to be found with a few other Christians in a little apartment at the back of the platform, pleading with God for blessing upon the meeting. Often as he emerged from this little sanctuary, his countenance revealed his tranquility of soul, and those present could not fail to realise that he had been enjoying a time of close fellowship with God. Indeed, as he mounted the three steps which led to the platform his very appearance proclaimed that he had come forth from the presence of God with a message for the people.

The eloquence and power with which he preached the Gospel this season was very marked, and throughout the whole series of meetings he maintained that calmness of spirit which had been so evident at the commencement.

Short after-meetings were held nightly, many of the Christians remaining behind to beseech the Lord for the salvation of souls, while others went amongst the unsaved pointing them to Christ.

Friday nights were devoted to testimony meetings, when many stood up and witnessed to the saving and keeping power of Christ. Several of these later devoted their entire time to the preaching of the Gospel in this and other lands.

The services were continued until the last week of November, when the tent was taken down and stored for the winter. The four months of continuous Gospel effort resulted in the salvation of many souls and the revival of the saints.

Chapter 20

CHAPEL FIELDS, 1908

The tent having been disposed of for the winter, he again resumed Sunday evening services in the various halls in the city, occasionally visiting Assemblies outside Belfast for the week-ends. He had still, however, a great love for tent-work, and the Chapel Fields, which had for so many years been the centre of blessing, once more attracted him. Consequently, at 10 a.m., on Sunday, 19th July, 1908, he held his first meeting, which he devoted to prayer and supplication to God for blessing upon the work. All Christians who had a heart for the work of God, and a desire for the propagation of the Gospel, were warmly invited to attend this meeting.

An afternoon service was held at four o'clock for Believers, and a Gospel meeting at 8.15. Large numbers attended both afternoon and evening services.

The Christians again felt delighted to have the privilege of associating with him for another season, and the unsaved listened with rapt attention, while he explained to them the necessity of the new birth and the plan of salvation.

His week-night services were held at the usual time, eight o'clock, on every evening, except Saturday.

The prayer-meeting at 10 a.m. on Sunday

mornings was held throughout this season, and greatly refreshed and stimulated the Christians in their service for God.

The Friday night testimony meetings were also resumed, and these too proved times of great blessing. It was most interesting to hear the testimonies of so many who had been brought to Christ through the work in the tent since it had first been erected in 1897.

On the last Lord's Day of October, when crossing the Ormeau Park to attend the morning prayer-meeting, he saw an ill-clad, rough-looking woman sleeping on one of the park seats. She had apparently been lying there for several hours, and as he sought to arouse her and speak to her about her soul, it occurred to him that he had for years been preaching to what was looked upon as a respectable class of people, but that this person represented a part of the community which he had seldom been able to reach with the Gospel. He continued on his way, pondering on this thought, when suddenly it flashed across his mind that if he followed the teaching of our Lord, and invited to a feast the maimed, the halt, the blind, and such as would come (see Luke 13) he should then have an opportunity of preaching the Gospel to them.

On arriving at the prayer-meeting he related his experience to some of the brethren, and explained his plan of reaching a class who had not hitherto been much sought after.

They heartily approved of the project, and it was arranged that at the meeting at four o'clock for Believers, a box should be placed at the door, so that all interested might have an opportunity of assisting this object by a free-will offering. Accordingly, at the afternoon meeting, he announced from the platform that a free tea would be provided for what might be termed the "outcasts of society," and that the Gospel would afterwards be preached; and invited all Christians who wished to have fellowship in this work and in the defraying of the expenses, to drop their offerings into the box placed at the tent door for that purpose.

The offering that day amounted to £16, and it was arranged that the "free tea" should be given on the following Friday. Twelve hundred tickets were printed and given the Christians to distribute amongst the very lowest and poorest class of people in the city.

Mr. George Stewart, of Ravenhill Road, Belfast, was the caterer for this and all subsequent teas.

The Christians voluntarily agreed to serve out the provisions to the audience, and on the 5th day of November eleven hundred of the poorest and most depraved people in the City of Belfast, irrespective of creed, were provided with a substantial meal, free of charge, in the old and famous circular tent.

After the tea, short Gospel addresses were delivered, and the meeting lasted for about an hour. The entire congregation listened, many perhaps for the first time, with rapt attention, while the old, old story of redeeming love was proclaimed.

This was the first of a series of nineteen free teas given during the next two and a half years. As the "show people" did not that year require the ground, he decided to continue the meetings through the winter and to provide free teas to the same class of people as often as funds allowed, and at each meeting to deliver Gospel addresses; arranging that no person should be permitted to leave the tent until the service was concluded.

Two weeks later a second tea was supplied to 1,200, and on the 4th December a further 1,200 partook of a similar repast. Again on the 29th of the month 1,320 were supplied with a substantial meal, and on January 15th and 28th, 1909, 800 and 700 respectively were provided with tea.

On the 11th February 600 outcasts assembled, and again availed themselves of the Christians' hospitality, and on the 4th of March, another tea was given at my father's instigation, and a further 600 poverty-stricken individuals attended and went away refreshed.

A Conference was held in the tent on the 17th March (St. Patrick's Day) for Believers, and refreshments were provied for 600 persons. This was a time of great blessing, and many were greatly helped and revived through the ministry at this meeting.

(Mr. Samuel Martin united with him in the work about this time, and continued to assist him until the year 1912, when he pitched the tent for the last time.)

Through the generosity of some kind Christian friends he was, on the 18th March, enabled to supply a further free tea to 600 of the poor of Belfast, and on the 7th of April, the 6th of May, and the 19th of the same month, 1,800 needy persons partook of the free meals under the canvas roof of his old tent. It is interesting to note, that his audience at every meeting included both maimed and blind, and on one occasion he referred in his address to the feast spoken of in Luke 13, and pointed out that every class named there was represented in this meeting.

CRUMLIN ROAD, BELFAST, 1909

This year he decided to pitch in another part of the city, and secured a piece of ground between the Crumlin and Oldpark Roads, close to Century Street, and at the rear of Mr. William Corbett's shop.

Mr. J. B. Ferguson kindly undertook to convey his tent from the Chapel Fields to this site, and when all arrangements had been completed and his tent pitched, he commenced his meetings.

His opening service, as usual, took the form of an address to Christians at four o'clock in the afternoon, and the usual Gospel meetings were held during the week.

These meetings were well attended, and many were brought to Christ during his mission in the tent in the summer of 1909. On one Lord's Day Mr. W. W. Fereday, of Uttoxeter, delivered an address to Christians at four o'clock in the afternoon, and spoke with great power to an audience numbering almost two thousand people.

He continued here during the greater part of the winter, and on the 15th and 29th of December he supplied free teas to 600 and 650 respectively, of the poor of this district, and in the months of January and February of 1910, 2,600 of these poor people partook of free meals in his well-heated and most comfortable tent. Thus he was able to preach the Gospel to the very poorest class, who were induced by the prospect of a good meal to attend the meetings, and who before leaving heard words whereby they might be saved. In one of these meetings a man was asked to come back on the following night, but he replied, "I can't come tomorrow night, as I have to go to mass, but will come back the next night."

On another occasion a little boy, who was selling firewood round the doors, said to a lady at one of the houses, "Please buy my last bundle, ma'am, I want to go to the tea-meeting in the tent."

During the period between November 5th, 1908, and February 23rd, 1910, he supplied fourteen thousand, three hundred, and seventy free meals, to the poorest and most degraded of Belfast, to all of whom he preached the Gospel in its simplicity, beseeching sinners to come to Christ, and to "flee from the wrath to come." Many of his audience had never before heard the story of God's redeeming love, and Eternity alone will reveal the results of these services.

CHAPEL FIELDS, 1910, 1911, and 1912

The ground upon which his tent was pitched on Crumlin Road being required for building purposes, he decided to return to his old site in the Chapel Fields. He did so, and held his first meeting here on the 4th August, 1910.

He continued until late in November, then had the tent taken down and stored until the following summer, when he again pitched it in the same place.

In the summer of 1912, he pitched in the Chapel Fields, for the last time. The tent, by this time, was so much worn that it was evident that it would be impossible to erect it again. It was pitiable to see the dilapidated state of the old canvas, which had been exposed to the sun for seven successive summers, had withstood the storms of several winters, and under the roof of which so many precious souls had passed "from death unto life."

The last service was held on the 10th November, and it was with much regret that he had the tent taken down and stored away.

Chapter 21

ULSTER HALL, BELFAST, 1913

His health, at this time, began to suffer from the strain of continuous work, and he was advised to take a rest, and not to embark again on so great an undertaking as the renewal of his large tent.

Early in 1913 he commenced a series of Sunday night meetings in the Ulster Hall, at 8.15 p.m. He carried on these services for about three months, and thousands attended during that period. He was assisted here by Mr. Martin, who had been closely associated with him in his labours for the previous four years.

MONKSTOWN, WHITEABBEY, 1913

This village is situated about seven miles from Belfast, and within two miles from Whiteabbey. The inhabitants are mostly factory-workers, and just that class of people who have frequently an open ear for the Gospel.

Messrs. Stephen and John Thompson (better known in Belfast as the "Thompson Brothers"), who followed their profession in the City and worked a Gospel tent in the summer, were conducting meetings in Monkstown at this time. They had been labouring in this place in 1912, and the Lord had so blessed their efforts and saved so many souls in the locality that they had decided to again pitch in the village.

My father, not having a tent this year, but still being desirous of preaching under canvas, especially where the Lord was working, expressed a wish that he might unite with them in the work.

These godly young men were delighted to have his help in the proclamation of the Gospel of our Lord Jesus Christ; and more so at a time when they were having such seasons of blessing.

He commenced with them on Lord's Day, the 3rd of August, and continued for two weeks, and these brethren state that they never heard him preach with greater power than he did while here.

It was a glorious sight to see almost eighty Christians form in procession, and march through this small village on a Sunday evening before the tent service commenced, singing praises to God, delivering short Gospel addresses, and inviting the people to the meetings. This was the sort of work that he loved, and the class of procession with which he delighted to be associated.

On one occasion he took for his subject Revelation 20:11-15, where "the dead small and great stand before the great White Throne, and whosoever's name is not found written in the book of life is cast into the Lake of Fire."

He pictured this scene with such awful reality, that the audience listened spell-bound, and the arrow of conviction penetrated into the hearts of many unsaved sinners.

Christians who were present at that meeting, and who had often heard him preach, state that they never before heard him speak with such awful solemnity and power as on that Sunday evening in Monkstown.

One interesting case of conversion was that of an old man, over seventy years of age, who was led to Christ while he was preaching. At the close of the address this old man came to him and said, "Tell Mr. Thompson I am saved." "Just tell him yourself" my father replied in his characteristic manner. He did so, and great was their rejoicing over the salvation of this precious soul.

Many young men who heard the Gospel at these meetings were, eighteen months afterwards, facing death on the battlefield.

Although he preached a great deal in Belfast and the neighbouring districts during the summer and winter of 1913, still the comparative rest from arduous and continuous labour had a good effect upon his health.

With the improvement of his health came the desire to launch a third large tent, and the matter having come under the notice of some of his friends, they decided to supply him with a tent in the summer of 1915. The war, however, breaking out in the meantime, and my father still being far from strong, the project was not carried out.

CROSSGAR, APRIL, 1914

On Saturday, the 25th of April, 1914, he attended a Conference of Christians, at Crossgar. Mr. Samuel Spence, of Belfast, Mr. W. W. Fereday, of England—who at that time was holding a series of meetings in Holborn Hall, Bangor—and my father were the principal speakers.

During the interval after the tea, he and a few friends walked along the Derryboye Road, and to them he related some of the experiences of his early years while preaching the Gospel in this part of the country. It was a beautiful afternoon, and he enjoyed the walk very much.

The Lord gave great liberty in the ministry at this small conference of about 120 Believers, and my father afterwards spoke with great delight of the happy fellowship he had with the Christians at that meeting.

ORMEAU ROAD GOSPEL HALL, BELFAST, 1914

During the summer he preached in Ormeau Road Gospel Hall for thirteen successive Sunday nights to large audiences and with great power. The saints were greatly refreshed through these meetings, and many later spoke of them as times of great blessing.

GALWAY (SECOND VISIT), 1914

I was labouring in the town of Galway in 1914, and was invited to preach in a hall belonging to a certain Protestant denomination in that place, but to my horror I found that some of my congregation held very strange views concerning the doctrine of eternal punishment.

As this was an evil which I believed required prompt and strong measures to counteract, especially in a place where there were very few Protestants, and fewer Christians, I wrote to my father to come to Galway at once, so that we might unitedly and earnestly contend for the Faith. Consequently, in the month of August of this year, he set out for the West, travelling from Belfast, via Dublin.

Shortly after the train left Broadstone Station, a man in the carriage, who had recently come from America, exclaimed several times in a loud voice, "Ireland! Ireland! Ireland!" "God loves Ireland," said my father; "and Dillon" said the stranger; "God loves Dillon," my father replied; "and Redmond," said the Irish-American; "yes, and Redmond, too," said my father; and added, "and God loves you. Have you ever thanked Him for it yet?" He then commenced preaching Christ to him, and the man became quite interested and listened most attentively.

The stranger, having reached the end of his journey, left the carriage, and another man entered; but he had not long been seated when my father said to him:— "Sir I have travelled two hundred miles on this journey, and no one has yet thought it worth while to ask me about my soul's eternal welfare." Thus he introduced the Gospel, which he faithfully preached to those in the carriage.

On his arrival at Galway I met him at the station, and we had a delightful time together. He told me he felt quite young and vigorous again, and longed to commence open-air work in places where the Gospel had never been preached.

On the following night he held his first meeting in Eyre Square. A large crowd of Roman Catholics attended, and listened attentively and reverently as he told them of the love of God, the atoning work of Christ, the necessity of the new birth, and warned them of the judgment of God which would surely fall upon all who rejected this great salvation. At the conclusion of this open-air service, he adjourned to a hall in the vicinity, where I had been holding some special meetings.

He spent a few days with me at my lodgings but, as he found some literature there which supported the very doctrine which he had come specially to oppose, he decided that we should obtain accommodation elsewhere.

After some difficulty we secured apartments in a Roman Catholic's house, where there were already several other boarders.

On our first night here, when about to partake of supper, he said to the company, "Before we take our food, we usually give thanks to God." A young, handsome girl, who was present, smiled rather sarcastically at this remark. After giving thanks, he spoke to her of the sacrifice of Christ, the love of God, and the beauties of Heaven, and when he had finished speaking, she exclaimed, with tears in her eyes, "What a lovely story!" The others at the table listened attentively and appeared deeply interested, and not one of them spoke a disparaging word of him or of his religion.

He preached in the Hall every night for a week, denouncing at each meeting the evil doctrine that had crept into some of the Protestant communities in Galway, proving from the Scriptures the Divinity of the Lord Jesus Christ, the Inspiration of the Word of God, and the eternal duration of the punishment of the wicked; with the result that a prominent member of one of the churches gathered up all the books he possessed which upheld the unsound doctrine, and made a huge bonfire of them in his yard. This member afterwards publicly declared that until the congregation denounced this heresy, he would disconnect himself from them. He carried his threat into execution by sending in his resignation, and thus one person at least was saved from the snare of the Evil One.

During the entire time we were in Galway, my father spoke about the things of God to every one with whom he came in contact. On one occasion while waiting for the tram-car, he observed a large poster on the wall of a building, with the words: "FORTY HOURS' EXPOSITION ON THE BLESSED COMMUNION IN ___ CHAPEL." A priest chanced to be passing on the opposite side of the street and, to my surprise, father beckoned him to come over. The priest crossed over to where we stood, and my father pointed to the poster and said, "What does that mean?" The priest very politely told him that the service would occupy several days, which would be devoted entirely to the exposition of the subject, and explained briefly to him the object of the proposed address. "And does it really take forty hours to explain the blessed communion?" enquired my father. "I take the communion, and it is most blessed indeed," he continued, "I take the bread, which reminds me of His body bruised for me, and I take the cup, which speaks of the blood that He shed, and which cleanseth from all sin." "Yes," said

the priest, "and it was all divine and voluntary."
They shook hands, and parted in a friendly manner,
and we rejoiced to hear such a profound confession
of the Divinity and sacrificial work of our Lord
Jesus Christ.

While he was here, we went one day to the town
of Oughterard, which is about twenty miles
distant, and held a meeting in the Market Square.
Several hundred attended this meeting in the open
air, and many stood in their door-way or looked out
from their window, as he proclaimed the Gospel in
its simplicity. Suddenly two donkeys, whose owners
had stopped to listen to his preaching, commenced
to bray loudly. Two old men, however, anxious that
he should not be disturbed, immediately tied ropes
round the jaws of the beasts, and thus saved him
from further interruption.

We returned to Galway, and on the following
Lord's Day evening he concluded his series of
meetings, at the close of which two gentlemen, who
had not previous to his coming paid much attention
to the erroneous doctrine, stood up and publicly
denounced the heresy. Their open declaration had a
great effect upon the audience, and caused some to
see the error of their ways.

A few days later we returned to Belfast. While on
the journey, three policemen, in charge of a
prisoner, entered the carriage. The poor fellow,
who was handcuffed, had a pipe in his mouth, and
asked my father for a match with which to light it.
He happened to be able to supply him, and said to
him in a sympathetic tone, "Just keep the pipe in
your mouth, and I'll light it for you." He did so, and

when the pipe had been lit, father, in his usual manner, seized the opportunity of speaking a word for God, and proceeded to tell the poor prisoner of the love of God for sinners, and of Christ's death on the Cross, and pleaded with him to accept Christ as his Saviour. "I remember," my father said, "when I was in the same position as you are, but God in His grace saved me, and has kept me ever since. I proved that 'the way of transgressors is hard,' but I have also proved that 'the path of the just is a shining light, that shineth more and more unto the perfect day'." The police and their charge listened attentively, but immediately he had finished speaking, an atheist, who was seated in the other corner of the carriage, drew from his pocket a book dealing with infidelity, and held it up before my father's face. Taking up his Bible and holding it before the eyes of the infidel, my father exclaimed, "What a difference!" The atheist put his book back into his pocket, without saying a word, and made no further attempt to interfere with him.

DRILL HALL, BELFAST, 1914

This Hall is situated on the Woodstock Road, and was built at the instance of the "Ulster Volunteer Force," for the purpose of training the members in military exercises.

In the winter of 1914 he rented this huge building, which seats over 2,000 people, and held meetings every Sunday night, at 8.15. These services were largely attended, the hall being filled at almost every meeting. A number were brought to Christ, and Christians of all denominations were greatly refreshed during this mission. Mr. Alexander Hamilton and Mr. W. H. McLaughlin assisted him in the proclamation of the Gospel here.

One Sunday afternoon he held a most interesting meeting, which was specially convened for "Ulster Volunteers." He announced as his subject, "Three Protestant Heroes," and delivered a most solemn address from the 1st, 2nd, and 3rd chapters of Daniel, dealing with the characteristics of Shadrach, Meshach, and Abednego. Many of those present on that occasion were, the following winter, fighting on the battlefields of Flanders, and elsewhere; and no doubt would well remember the solemn Gospel message which they had heard on that Lord's Day afternoon in the Drill Hall at Belfast.

Chapter 22

VALE OF AVOCA, COUNTY WICKLOW

LIMERICK AND COUNTY CLARE, 1915

In the summer of 1915, he visited County Wicklow, and travelled through the Vale of Avoca, distributing tracts, speaking to people individually, and preaching where he could obtain a house or building in which to hold a meeting. He visited all the public-houses en route, and gave Gospel literature to the publicans and barmen, and spoke to all with whom he came in contact about the necessity of the new birth.

He held a few meetings in a church in the district, and on the first night, the clergyman, who always kept strictly to the hour for closing the service, seemed a little annoyed when he exceeded the time, and anxiously looked at his watch.

My father, of course, observed this, but did not mention the matter until the following night, when, after he had been speaking for some time, he looked round the building and said, "I see there is no clock in this church, and we don't need any, nor do we need watches; so we will just go on here, as the Lord may help us."

I was at this time labouring in the West of Ireland, having travelled through the counties of Mayo, Galway, and Clare; and while in the latter place, I wrote to him to come to Limerick and I should meet him there. He did so, and a dear servant of the Lord in that city placed his motor car at his disposal and accompanied him on a tour through the counties of Limerick and Clare. By this means they travelled over two hundred miles, my father making good use of his time by preaching Christ whenever opportunity offered.

On one occasion I accompanied him to the top of the Doonbeg Hill, which commands a splendid view of the surrounding district within a circuit of about twenty miles. Small farms and labourers' cottages were to be seen dotted thickly over the landscape, and as we stood gazing upon them, he remarked, "Tom, you have a big parish, I would like to go with you to carry the Gospel into the homes of these superstitious West of Ireland people."

TULLYBOY, COUNTY CAVAN, 1915

At this time, in consequence of my wife's delicate health, I was obliged to return home for a short period, and on the 29th September we went from Belfast to a Believers' Conference, which was to be held at Mr. Gordon's, of Tullyboy. My father journeyed in the side-car of my bicycle, and took with him a supply of tracts, which he distributed freely amongst the inhabitants of the villages through which we passed, and also to the pedestrians whom we met on the way.

Occasionally, when approaching a house, he would request me to stop so that he might have an opportunity of speaking to the occupants. Being in feeble health, he was so wrapped up for the journey that scarcely anything but his eyes was visible and, as he was covered with dust, he presented such an appearance that the people came out, eager to know who we were; and as they walked inquiringly around the bicycle, he would follow them with his eyes, preaching Christ and handing tracts to them.

During this journey of 140 miles, there was scarcely one with whom we conversed who did not receive from him a message concerning Eternal things.

He enjoyed this tour immensely, and said he felt quite young again when at such work, and expressed a keen desire to accompany me on my next visit to the West, which I contemplated making in the following summer. He afterwards spoke of his visit to Mr. Gordon's as a time of great refreshing to his soul, and was delighted at the prospect of once more going forth into out-of-the-way places, to carry the Gospel to districts where it had seldom before been preached.

During the winter of 1915, although he was in a very poor state of health, he visited Magherafelt, Coleraine, and several other places, conducting short missions for a few days at a time. But early in 1916, his health so entirely failed him that he was obliged to remain at home practically all the time, and to confine his travels to places at short distances, where it would not be necessary for him to remain overnight. Thus had he to submit to the demands of a constitution undermined by over-exertion, and of a weak body well-nigh worn out in the Master's service. Truly the spirit was willing, but the flesh weak.

HIS LAST PUBLIC GOSPEL SERVICE
BANGOR, COUNTY DOWN, 1916

On the invitation of Mr. Robert M'Clay, who had for many years been one of his most ardent friends, he readily consented to preach the Gospel in the Central Hall, Bangor. The meeting was duly announced for Sunday, the 12th of March, 1916, and at the hour appointed to commence, the hall was packed.

He took for his subject the story of Esau selling his birthright for a mess of pottage, Genesis 25:30-34, and with soul-stirring pathos, he besought his unsaved hearers not to barter their soul's salvation for the vanities of this life, or perhaps for only a few hours of worldly pleasure.

He depicted in eloquent language the grandeur of the heavenly mansions which the Christ of God has gone to prepare for all those who have accepted Him as their Saviour, and described the thrilling joys and eternal pleasures which those who trust Him shall enter upon when the "earthly house of this tabernacle is dissolved." He pointed out that, ere the meeting closed, the heavens might open, and the Lord Himself descend in majestic splendour, and with a shout, with the voice of the Archangel and the trump of God, awaken the myriads of saints who for thousands of years have been in their tombs, and that we, the living saints, with them should triumphantly ascend to be for ever with the Lord.

With this he contrasted the awful horrors of an endless Hell, and the millions upon millions of years of sorrow and remorse in store for those who refuse God's offer of mercy, and die without Christ: their birthright sold for "a mess of pottage," their souls lost, and they banished from the presence of God into that awful abyss of woe, with the wailing cry of despair upon their lips, "The harvest is past, the summer is ended, and I am not saved."

The power of God was felt in a marked degree, and the audience was held spell-bound, as with solemn earnestness, he pleaded with the unsaved to accept Christ as their Saviour, and with pathetic tenderness warned them to flee from the wrath to come. The whole service, indeed, was befitting this occasion, as in the Providence of God, this was the last public address which he ever delivered.

At the close of the meeting, he sang that beautiful hymn:—

Have you read the story of the Cross
　Where Jesus bled and died?
Where your debt was paid by His precious
　　blood,
　That flowed from His wounded side?

Chorus:

He died of a broken heart for thee.
　He died of a broken heart.
Oh! wondrous love, it was for thee
　He died of a broken heart.

Have you read how they placed the crown of
    thorns
    Upon His lovely brow?
When He prayed, "Forgive them, Oh; forgive,
    They know not what they do."

Have you read how He saved the dying thief,
    When hanging on the tree?
Who looked with pitying eyes and said,
    "Dear Lord, remember me."

Have you heard that he looked to Heaven and
    said,
    "'Tis finished"?—it was for thee.
Have you ever said, "I thank Thee, Lord,
    For giving Thy life for me?"

The brethren connected with the Assembly were
so much impressed with his preaching that they
invited him to conduct the Gospel service on the
following Lord's Day evening, preliminary to his
commencing a series of meetings in this hall.

During the week, however, he became so ill that
he was confined to bed, and from this illness he
never fully recovered.

He afterwards spoke often of that meeting in
Bangor, and said that, if the Lord enabled him to
take up Gospel work again, he would like to
commence in that town.

Little did he, or those who were present that
night think, as he descended from the platform, at
about 7.45 on the evening of the 12th day of March,
1916, that he would never again ascend a public

platform, nor tell to the lost and perishing, in a
public hall, the "Old, old, story of Jesus and His
love," which he had during his forty-seven years'
ministry proclaimed within the hearing of thousands
of his fellow-travellers to eternity.

Chapter 23

HIS LAST ILLNESS

ANTRIM ROAD, BELFAST, APRIL TO JULY, 1916

As he gradually grew weaker, my sister not being very strong, he decided to take furnished apartments, and thus relieve her from the worry of household duties. He secured these in the house of a nice family on the Antrim Road. Here he became so weak that eventually he was confined to bed. At this time I was labouring in Ballina, County Mayo, and my sister wrote asking me to come home. On my arrival at Belfast, I went to see my father and expressed my sorrow at finding him so ill. "I am very ill in body, Tom," he said, "but Christ is becoming more precious to me every day. A restored soul is more to be desired than a restored body."

He then enquired about my work in the West, and did not seem satisfied until I had related in detail all the incidents in connection with my mission in Achill Island, Westport, and other places which I had visited. He interrupted me several times with exclamations of delight, as I told him of occasions when the Lord had put forth His hand in the saving of souls, or when He had delivered me out of difficulties. He was always greatly interested in my work in the West and I believe, that had he lived, I should often have had him with me in this needy part of Ireland.

I had a bed placed in his room, and stayed with him every night for five weeks. Often he had weak turns, and at such times he thought the end was near, but I always encouraged him to believe, as I then myself believed, that he would recover.

One night he was much worse than usual, and in his weakness he said, "Tom, the end is coming soon." "Do not think that, father," I replied, "You will be all right again." A Christian lady called to see him the following day, and when speaking of his severe illness on the previous night, she said, "I do not think the Lord will call you home yet, Mr. Rea." "You're like Tom," he replied, "Tom won't let me die at all."

While he was here, many of his old friends and associates visited him, among whom were Dr. W. J. Matthews and Mr. T. R. Prentice, of Belfast, also Mr. Ramsay, of Lurgan, all of whom had happy fellowship with him as they sat by his bedside, conversing about the things of God.

During the Easter Conference held in Belfast, several of the speakers called upon him, among whom were Mr. McLay, of Cardiff, and Mr. Hanley Bird, of India, and they, too, although very sorrowful indeed to find him so weak, rejoiced to see him so tranquil in spirit and so happy in the Lord. At the Conference, reference was made to his peaceful state of mind and joyful condition of soul as he lay upon what was believed to be his deathbed.

When visiting him, Mr. M'Lay, of Cardiff, asked him if he had any message for the meeting, and he replied, "Tell them that I have been just revelling in the twenty-third Psalm, especially the portion: 'The Lord is my Shepherd; I shall not want. He maketh me to lie down in green pastures; He leadeth me beside the still waters. He restoreth my soul'."

Although resigned to the will of his Lord and Master, he still had the desire to embark upon the work of the Gospel again, should he recover. He said to a Christian friend and his wife, who frequently visited him, that, if God enabled him to preach again, he hoped to do so more faithfully than ever before. They stated that they would pray for his recovery, which greatly encouraged him, and he expressed extreme delight at the thought of being able to be up and at the work again.

To a Christian friend, who visited him in the month of May and reminded him of the Conference in Dromore, which was to be held on the following day, he said, "Remember me to those in Dromore, and ask them to pray to God that He may restore my health, as, if it is His will, I should like to preach in that little town again."

Towards the beginning of June he had so far recovered as to be able to sit for a short time in the drawing-room, and by the end of the month he had become so much better that some of his friends thought they would soon hear him again proclaiming the Gospel from the public platform.

BANGOR, JULY, 1916

With the improvement of health there came the desire for a change of air, and it was arranged that he should go to Bangor, a residential watering-place about twelve miles from Belfast, on the County Down side of the Lough. Apartments having been secured in a nicely situated house on the Seacliffe Road, he went there on the first day of July.

He had hoped to be strong enough to walk along the shore, so armed himself with a large quantity of Gospel tracts, which he called his "ammunition," and which he intended to distribute among the large crowds who frequent this place during the summer months.

While at Bangor his health improved a little. As he was still, however, too weak to walk, he procured a bath-chair, and was thus able to reach the shore, where he distributed Gospel literature among the numerous visitors.

During his stay in Bangor, Mrs. Gibson, of Belfast, who had for many years been a warm friend of his, visited him almost every day. She still speaks of the happy fellowship which they enjoyed together, and of how refreshed she often was after these periods of conversing on spiritual matters.

Towards the end of the month he became much better, and during his last week there was able to drive out, on four different occasions, for long distances with some friends.

SPA, BALLYNAHINCH, AUGUST, 1916

He had twice previously, after severe illnesses, been greatly benefited in health by residence at the Spa, Ballynahinch, and he now expressed a desire once more to visit this place. Having secured a house here for the month of August, Mr. Dawson Cotton, an esteemed brother in the Lord, who had made arrangements for his apartments at Bangor, also kindly interested himself in seeing him comfortably settled at the Spa. They left Bangor on Monday, the 31st of July, and motored to Bally-nahinch, which is about twenty miles distant.

During his first week at the Spa, he continued to improve, and so much better had he become that he decided to pay a visit to Mr. James Ferguson, of Growell, who had been for many years one of his most intimate friends.

Mrs. Moffat, of Ballynahinch, had kindly under-taken to have him conveyed to Growell, which is a distance of about eight miles, in her motor, but on the morning appointed, just as he was about to step into the car, he felt so ill that he was unable to go. He appeared disappointed, and said in a somewhat sad tone of voice, "No driving for me today."

He grew weaker and weaker, and my sister again wrote for me. I arrived on the 21st of August, and as I entered his bedroom, he said, "Tom, you're just in time. Not a minute too soon and not a minute too late." He then said, "Now, Tom, what about the work in Sligo?" I talked with him about this for some time, and then enquired, "Is there anything you want me to do, father?" "All I want you to do is to sit by my side," he replied. I remained with him, and he was very restless that night, tossing about on his bed and sleeping very little.

Next day, however, he appeared a little better, and after I had read and prayed with him, he said, "What a comfort it is to have you by my side! The

Lord just sent you in time."

He was again very restless that night, and appeared to be suffering great pain. In the morning he looked somewhat depressed, and when I had read a portion of the Scriptures, I said to him, "Father, I want to read you a few pages of a little book named 'Daniel Quorm,' relating to his conversation with a dying saint called 'Frank Vivian'."

I commenced at the place where Frank related the conflict he had had with the Tempter on the previous night. I read how Satan had taunted him with the thought that God did not love him, and how Frank, in order to prove God's love, had taken his enemy first to Gethsemane, where the Lord in His agony "sweat as it were great drops of blood," and then to the Judgment Hall, where he stood bound and forsaken, before Pilate's Bar, and from thence to Calvary, where He bled and died. Here Frank cries, "Look, Tempter. Canst thou see my own Blessed Lord hanging on the Cross for me, bleeding, torn, dying, for my soul? That is how He loves me. He gave Himself for me. In the face of this, canst thou say that He does not love me?" "I turned round," states Frank, "to see what the old Tempter thought of that, but when I looked he had gone, clean gone. I don't believe he can set foot on Calvary's Hill, so I mean to keep under the Cross, right under the Cross, out of his road, and it's a wonderful shelter, a beautiful place, hid in the Cleft of the Rock." When I reached this point my father exclaimed, "Hallelujah! Praise the Lord! That's where I was last night, Tom. Wonderful, wonderful, that you have read that to me this morning. Calvary, Calvary, dark Calvary, blessed Calvary! It was there that Jesus died for me. Oh, the Blood, the precious Blood, shed on Calvary's Cross for me! Victory, victory, victory through the Blood of the Lamb that was slain!" With such language as this, he revelled for the rest of the day in the thought of Christ's death on the Cross for him.

As he desired to get back to Belfast, we arranged that he should enter a nursing-home in the City, and Mr. Cotton engaged a motor laudelette for the purpose of having him conveyed there. He was so weak, however, that it was considered unsafe to have him removed. During the week, Mr. James Johnston, of Liscard, Liverpool, having heard that he was ill, called to see him, and my father's delight at seeing this old, esteemed friend was great.

After this his joy seemed to increase, and often, when lying upon his bed, he would break forth in raptures and cry out, "My beautiful Lord, my precious Saviour! To think that Thou wouldst suffer on the Cross for me! The Cross, the Cross, dark Calvary, where my beautiful Jesus died for sinful me! Oh, the blood, that Jesus shed for me! Mocked, scourged, crucified for me!"

On the day before he died, knowing that the end was near, I said to him, "Father, it will be grand to be where there is no death." "No death, no death, Tom," he repeated, "Why, this is the best time I have ever had in my life." A little later he said, "The harvest is past, Tom," (meaning that there would be no more "bringing in of the sheaves" for him). "The sands of time are sinking. Sweet the moments rich in blessing. Victory, victory, victory, through the blood of my precious Lord, Who loved me and gave Himself for me! Just to think that I am lying outside the gate! Is it wrong for me to wish an entrance? Pray, Tom, that I may soon get in." Some time afterwards he said, "Poor Fann," referring to my sister Fanny, who was a mere infant when my mother died, and whom he had loved and cherished from her childhood. "Don't worry about Fanny, father," I said, "for as long as I live, she shall be provided for." The troubled look which for a moment had overshadowed his face, fled; and, looking up with an expression of delight, he said, "Thank you, Tom."

"Father," I said to him, "Do you remember the time you were at Ougherard, when you sang that beautiful hymn to over three hundred Roman Catholics in the Square?" "What hymn was that?" he enquired. "His grace is sufficient for me," I replied.

He immediately clasped his hands as in the attitude of prayer, and sang with such a clear, musical, and sweet voice as I have never before heard, the first verse of the hymn, which is as follows:—

His grace was sufficient for me,
　　When in trembling and fear,
　　To His side I drew near,
　　And He cleansed me from sin,
　　Made my heart pure within,
His grace was sufficient for me.

For me, for me, His grace is sufficient for me,
His grace is sufficient for me.

When he had sung these words, he said to me,
"What is the next verse, Tom?" I had quite
forgotten it, and replied, "I don't know, father." He
looked up and said, "You should never forget that
hymn." I was so affected that I went downstairs and
said to my sister, "Fanny, go up to Father, and enjoy
a little bit of Heaven." As she entered his room, she
heard him exclaim in a clear, strong, voice,
"Glorious Mount Calvary! My precious Lord that
loved me! My blessed Redeemer!" His rapture was
great, and he appeared to be enjoying a real
foretaste of Heaven. As Fanny looked upon him,
she saw that he would soon be inside the portals of
the heavenly City, and at the thought of parting
with him, she was so overcome with grief that she
left the room, and on coming downstairs she
exclaimed, amidst her tears, "What a sight! He is
awfully happy."

The remaining verses of the hymn are as
follows:—

His grace is sufficient for me;
    And, whatever my lot,
    I can hear His "Fear not."
    I am safe in His care,
    Who can guard from each snare:
His grace is sufficient for me.

His grace is sufficient for me;
   All my need He'll provide,
   And my steps homeward guide;
   And in death I shall sing,
   As I rest 'neath His wing,
"His grace is sufficient for me."

His grace is sufficient for me,
   When in mansions of bliss,
   Still my theme shall be this;
   And for aye I shall sing
   In the praise of my King,
Whose grace is sufficient for me.

I might here state that he learned this hymn about six years previously. In the autumn of 1910, when spending an evening at Mrs. Gibson's, Belfast, it was sung by her daughter, May. It immediately attracted him, and he requested her to sing it again. They sang it several times and, before he left, he said, "Now I have it. It will be a solo for me as long as I live." Strange indeed, that it should be his last song on earth and that he should sing it with such melody.

The following day, which was his last on earth, he was somewhat restless in the forenoon. He asked me to pray that the Lord would give him rest and enable him to sleep. I did so, and shortly afterwards, he fell into a calm repose, and throughout the day he had seasons of great rapture.

A short time before his home-call, he said "Good-bye" to his nurse, who had been most attentive to him, and had often sat by his bedside reading to him his favourite hymns. A few minutes before he passed away, I whispered to him the words, "What a friend we have in Jesus!" "Yes," he faintly replied, "the best Friend on earth." Thus at a quarter to seven, on the evening of the 2nd September, 1916, he calmly and peacefully departed to be for ever with the Lord.

Chapter 24

FUNERAL

Soon afterwards I journeyed to Belfast, which is 17 miles distant, in order to inform some friends of his death, and to attend to some matters in connection with the funeral. While there I called upon Mr. Gibson, who kindly undertook to look after the funeral arrangements, and have them carried out in accordance with my wishes. This was a great relief to me, in consequence of the inconvenience of travelling to and from Ballynahinch.

A Christian friend who, with his wife, spent the following night with us at the Spa, states that he shall never forget that Lord's Day evening. Before retiring to rest, we visited the room where all that was mortal of my father lay, and as we gazed upon his face, which in the feeble light looked as though he were in a pleasant sleep, and which bore a distinct expression of joyful surprise, I said to my friend, "He just looks as if he were going to open his eyes, and tell us of something beautiful that he had seen." As we stood in that silent death chamber on that lovely autumn evening, with the refreshing breeze blowing in through the half-open window, and the leaves rustling on the trees outside, as if almost hushed in silence, my friend uttered these words, "Let me die the death of the righteous, and let my last end be like his."

We arranged that the funeral should take place
on the following Tuesday, September 5th, leaving
the Spa at 10 a.m., where a service would be
conducted before starting for my home at 88
Ravenscroft Avenue, Belfast; and that a further
service should be held there, the funeral procession
to leave my house at 1 p.m., travelling to
Portadown, which is twenty-five miles from Belfast,
via Lisburn and Lurgan.

As the journey was long, the route traversed
being about forty-three miles, we decided that
opportunity could only be given for one speaker at
each service.

Our aged brother, Mr. Samuel Martin, took the
service at the Spa, and delivered a very solemn
address to those who had assembled there to pay
their last tribute of respect to one most dearly
loved. Some of his hearers were unsaved, and his
words were most appropriate.

The friends who attended at the Spa were
conveyed to Belfast in motor-cars, where we
arrived about twelve o'clock. A large number of
people had assembled at the house, and on our
arrival we had the coffin-lid removed, so that his
friends might look upon him for the last time. Many
tears were shed as they left the room where his
body lay.

We had hoped that Mr. Henry Pickering, of
Glasgow, who was a very highly-esteemed friend of
my father's, would conduct the service at Belfast,
but, being ill at that time, he wired that he was
unable to do so.

Mr. W. H. McLaughlin, however, took the service

here, and as the day was fine, he spoke from a chair outside the door, to over one thousand people, who had congregated around the house and in the vicinity. He, too, spoke with great power, and delivered a very appropriate Gospel message to this great audience. Both at the commencement and close of the service, one of my father's favourite hymns was sung, the words of which are as follows:—

In the land of fadeless day,
    Lies the "City Four-square";
It shall never pass away,
    And there is "no night there."

God shall "wipe away all tears,"
    There's no death, no pain, nor fears;
And they count not time by years,
    For there is "no night there."

All the gates of pearl are made,
    In the "City Four-square";
All the streets with gold are laid,
    And there is "no night there."

And the gates shall never close,
    To the "City Four-square";
There life's crystal river flows,
    And there is "no night there."

There they need no sunshine bright,
    In the "City Four-square";
For the Lamb is all the light,
    And there is "NO NIGHT THERE."

The funeral cortege left Ravenscroft Avenue about 1.20 p.m., and travelled across the City for about one and a half miles, during which time a slight rain fell, although the earlier part of the day had been very fine. We intended that sufficient motor-cars should be provided to convey all those who desired to accompany the funeral, and this having come to the knowledge of our Christian friends, a number of them brought their cars the whole way. Among these were Mr. W. H. McLaughlin, Mr. A. Hamilton, Mr. R. D. Gordon, Mr. F. Mawhinney, Mr. R. Bothwell, and was Dr. Darling. Several others hired cars, so that accommodation provided for all.

After we left Belfast the rain ceased, and the roads were in splendid condition for motoring. In this we saw the hand of the Lord, even in causing it to rain, as otherwise, with twenty motors in succession, a tremendous amount of dust would have been raised, which would have made it very unpleasant for those in the cars.

At Lurgan a number of friends, with horse-drawn vehicles, joined us, and from there we drove slowly until within about a mile of Portadown, when all dismounted and the entire procession walked to the grave-side.

All along the route between Lurgan and Portadown, which was my father's native place, the roads were lined with people, who stood with bowed heads as the cortege passed.

We arrived at the cemetery at 4.5 p.m., just five minutes later than the time arranged.

Mr. Burnett, of Portadown, had kindly seen to

the opening of the grave. My father had before his death expressed the wish that Mr. W. H. McLaughlin should take the service at the grave-side, and he delivered a most solemn address to a large number, who stood around the open grave. He spoke of the sweet fellowship he had enjoyed with my father in Gospel work, for over forty years, and warned the unsaved of the consequences of neglecting their soul's salvation.

My father's favourite hymn, "The City Four-Square," was also sung here, and Dr. Darling closed with prayer.

All that was mortal of my beloved father was then interred "in sure and certain hope of a glorious resurrection at the coming of our Blessed Lord and Saviour, Jesus Christ." It was with heavy hearts and sorrowful faces that my brother, Meredith, and myself left Seagoe Cemetery that afternoon in September; but how blessed it is to remember that "He that cometh shall come, and shall not tarry." Till then, let us "occupy till He come," and, stretching forward to the things that are before," let us "press on toward the goal unto the prize of the high calling of God in Christ Jesus."

Chapter 25

APPENDIX

His long and arduous labours in the Gospel secured for him the esteem of many who knew him, and even those who were not associated with him in his religious work admired his perseverance and zeal.

The *Belfast Evening Telegraph*, in its issue of the 4th September, 1916, contributes a somewhat lengthy article to his memory, from which the following is an extract:—

DEATH OF MR. DAVID REA

ZEALOUS BELFAST EVANGELIST

A noted figure in the religious and evangelistic life of Belfast has been removed by the death of Mr. David Rea, who passed away on Saturday, at Echo Cottage, Spa, Ballynahinch, whither he had gone in declining health a few weeks ago. The late Mr. Rea spent practically the entire of a long lifetime in the proclamation of the Gospel to the people in tents, and halls, and open spaces, and the delivery of his message was followed by results that were cheering to himself and those associated with him in the work.

A native of the Portadown district, he was early the subject of religious influences, and became an active Christian worker. He was formerly connected with the Irish Evangelisation Society, an un-denominational agency, labouring under the direction of the late Mr. Barton, Dundalk. Later, he was more intimately associated with "the Brethren," although, in the evangelistic work to which his life was dedicated, his labours were more personal than under the wing of any religious organisation.

Mr. Rea generally preached in a large tent seating 2,000 people, where he invariably attracted crowded congregations. It was for many years pitched in the Chapel Fields, but, in addition, he successfully pursued his evangelistic labours in Dublin and other parts of Ireland, and also in Liverpool and Glasgow. During some winters the late evangelist spoke on successive Sunday evenings to large gatherings in the Ulster Hall. His missions frequently attracted members of the non-church going masses, while his philanthropic enterprises extended themselves to free repasts to the poorest of the folk in the neighbourhood where his tent was located.

Mr. Rea was a man of many natural gifts; he was a fluent speaker, a keen Bible student, and as full of zeal and fire as a prophet of old. He had a wonderful influence over many minds, and his lifework left its impress on multitudes of people."

Mr. Henry Pickering, of Glasgow, editor of *The Witness*, also devotes a full page of his journal of October, 1916, to a revision of my father's labours in the Gospel, under the title of "Home-call of a Warrior," from which I have culled the following:—

"Two men — and two only — out of all the great

preachers whom we have heard during the last half-century, have had that peculiar 'unction' which, for want of a more definite term, might be described as 'Spiritual electricity.'

The first was Richard Weaver — a greater God-made preacher has not been known in living memory. The moment he began to speak — at least in his palmy days — he sent a power and reality through the hearts of the thousands who thronged to hear him. You felt God was there. The Spirit was working. The Bleeding Lamb, of whom he loved to sing, was the centre, and eternal issues were at stake.

The other was DAVID REA, who was also endued with this peculiar power. Twenty-five years ago, and earlier, when Mr. Rea was in the full vigour of manhood, it was well worth walking ten miles any night to hear his burning words of Gospel Grace flowing forth with natural eloquence — a spiritual penetration, a deepening intensity, and a soul-convicting, soul-awakening, and soul-converting force, which we have never seen equalled in our Gospel Halls, before or since.

During the last twenty years, he worked more or less with monster tents, increasing in size until, at times, he had an audience of three thousand persons under canvas. Thousands thereby heard the 'Old, Old, Story,' and hundreds were led to the feet of the Master and Lord, whose glory was the centre of his efforts.

He died on September 2nd, at the Spa, Bally-nahinch, and the brethren gathered in large numbers to manifest their respect for this earnest devotion and sincerity.

At Ballynahinch, Belfast, Lisburn, Lurgan, and at the grave-side, Portadown, a large concourse of mourners sorrowed, yet not as those without hope, knowing —

"That death and darkness and the tomb,
Only pain us till He come."

Mr. James Stephens, of Paisley, too, writes a beautiful article of him in the "Believers' Pathway," of October, 1916; and Mr. John Ritchie, of Kilmarnock, who preached with him on several occasions in his large tent in the Chapel Fields, Belfast, pays high tribute, in his Magazines of the same date, to the interesting career of my beloved father.

THE TESTIMONY OF ONE WHO WAS SAVED THROUGH HIS MINISTRY IN 1876

There are few assemblies in the North of Ireland which have not amongst them some who were converted through the instrumentality of my father, and, in the different churches and Mission Halls, numbers may be found who have been saved at his meetings. Indeed in many parts of the world there are still living aged Christians who can date their conversion to the time when they were led, through his preaching, to accept Christ as their Saviour.

Mr. James Moore, of Liverpool, tells of his coming to Magherafelt in the year 1876, and of how the inhabitants of the district were filled with amazement at the "wonderful preacher," as he was called. He states: When I was a lad, about 19 years of age, I was asked to drive Mr. Rea on an Irish jaunting-car, to a meeting. There were a few other Christians on the car, and Mr. Rea must have thought I was anxious about my soul, for, as soon as we started on our journey, he began to sing that hymn:

"There is life for a look at the Crucified One,
There is life at this moment for thee:
Then look, sinner, look unto Him and be saved,
Unto Him who was nailed to the tree."

I drove on as rapidly as I could to get the journey over, lest he should enter into personal conversation with me. The hymn, however, kept ringing in my ears, and when we arrived at the hall, I went inside, although I had not intended to do so.

I can well remember the Scripture from which he preached that night. It was Mark 2 verse 3: "And they came unto Him, bringing one sick of the palsy, which was borne of four." He pictured the helpless condition of the poor man, unable to do anything for himself, and pointed out that sin had so paralysed all the sons of Adam's race that they could do nothing to help themselves, and that, so far as their ability to redeem their own souls was concerned, they were just in the same state as the man spoken of in Mark 2. He further pointed out that, although they were spiritually paralysed, with the wrath of God abiding on them, the Lord Jesus Christ had power on earth to forgive sins and to quicken dead souls, and that He still received sinful men.

With pathetic tenderness in his dear, penetrating voice, he pleaded with the unsaved to accept Christ as their Saviour, and while he was speaking I was awakened to see my true position before God. I realised that I was a guilty sinner, and that Jesus had borne my sins in His own body on the tree; and that night I trusted Him and passed from death unto life.

After I was saved, I asked Mr. Rea what I should say to my companions, of whom there were five or six. "Just tell them at once that you are converted," he replied. I did so the following evening, and some of them said that I had gone "religiously mad." I spoke to them about their souls, but I found that afterwards they had no desire for my company; thus I could say, "My old companions, fare you well."

It is now 40 years since this happened, and I have proved that the Lord Jesus Christ is not only able to save, but is also able to keep.

I have blessed God thousands of times since, that ever I entered that little school-house to hear this "wonderful preacher."

Chapter 26

JEHOVAH-JIREH

(THE LORD WILL PROVIDE)

My father was invited to preach in a certain place which was a considerable distance from his home. On the morning, when he was about to start on his journey, he found that he had not the wherewithal to pay his train fare; in fact, he had only one halfpenny in his possession. He prayed to God that, if it were His will that he should go, He would provide him with the means for the journey; after which he put on his hat, took umbrella and bag in hands, and set out for the train, with only the halfpenny in his pocket. When about half-way to the station, he met a gentleman, who expressed his delight at seeing him, and gave him a cheque for several pounds.

A STRANGE AWAKENING

Early one winter's morning he was passing through a village in the County Armagh, and as he entered the Main Street, he was led to sing that beautiful hymn:

The blast of the trumpet, so loud and so shrill,
Will shortly re-echo o'er ocean and hill.

Chorus:-
When the mighty, mighty, mighty trump sounds,
  "Come, come away,"
Oh, sinner, be ready to hail the glad day.

The earth and the waters will yield up their dead,
The righteous with joy will awake from their bed.

The chorus of angels will burst from the skies,
And blend with the shout of the saints as they rise.

The cry of the Bridegroom will echo around,
And the Bride in her beauty go forth at the sound.

Acknowledged by Jesus, confessed as His own,
Transported to Glory, we'll sit on His throne.

When the mighty, mighty, mighty, trump sounds,
  "Come, come away,"
Oh, sinner, be ready to hail the glad day.

Slowly he marched up the street in the stillness of
the early dawn, his melodious, strong voice
resounding from end to end of the village, and re-
echoing in startling tones as he raised the loud
notes of the chorus:—

When the mighty, mighty, mighty trump sounds,
  "Come, come away,"
Oh, sinner, be ready to hail the glad day.

As he moved along, many windows were opened,
and many eyes peered out into the darkness to see
the cause of this strange noise.

Twenty years had run their course and he had almost forgotten the incident, when at the close of one of his tent services in the Chapel Fields, a man came to him and enquired if he remembered passing through a village early one morning singing the hymn, "The blast of the trumpet so loud and so shrill, shall shortly re-echo o'er ocean and hill." My father replied that he did. "Well," said he, "You awoke me out of my sleep that morning, and as I heard you sing, 'When the mighty, mighty, mighty trump sounds, come, come away, Oh, sinner, be ready to hail the glad day,' I thought the Judgment Day had come, and I was not ready. This was the means of awakening me to think about my soul, and shortly afterwards I was led to accept Christ as my Saviour. I have since been in America, and am only a short time home, and I'm very glad to meet you tonight."

ANSWERED PRAYER

On one occasion he required the sum of £50 to discharge an account which had been contracted in connection with his work in the Gospel. Two days before it became due, he felt led to pray that the Lord would influence a certain Scotch brother who was well-off, to send him the necessary amount. On the morning that the bill was to be paid, he was overjoyed to receive a letter from this very brother, enclosing a cheque for £50. Thus the Lord answered prayer, and he was enabled to meet his obligation. "Be careful for nothing, but in everything by prayer and supplication, with thanksgiving, let your requests be made known unto God." Phil. 4:6.

IS IT RIGHT TO PAY YOUR DEBT?

He was ever seeking an opportunity to witness for God under all circumstances, and when travelling by rail on one occasion, he introduced the Gospel to the occupants of the carriage by inquiring of a man seated opposite him, "Is it right for a man to pay his debt?" "Yes," the gentleman replied, "All men should pay their debts." "Well," said my father, "I am a debtor to you." "I am not aware of your owing me any money," answered the man in surprise. "Well, I am a debtor to 'both the wise and the unwise,' and you belong to one of these two classes; therefore I am a debtor to you," was my father's reply, and from this text, Romans 1:14, he preached the Gospel to the entire company.

"HOW MUCH WOULD YOU TAKE FOR THE WORST OF YOUR CHILDREN?"

On another occasion, when in the train, a lady in the carriage had three rather noisy and unruly boys with her. She had called them to order several times, but they appeared uncontrollable, and when she had at length scolded them severely, my father, anxious to introduce the Gospel, said to her, "Madam, how much would you take for the worst of these children, say, this boy here?" pointing to one whom he had noticed was a little more troublesome than the others. "Oh, I wouldn't sell any of them," she replied. "But you surely cannot care anything about this little rascal?" "Yes," she answered, "I love this child as much as any of them." "Then," he said, "in this respect you are just like God. For He loved me when I was wayward and bad, and many years ago I accepted Christ as my Saviour, and now I know my sins forgiven." In this way, he preached the glorious Gospel of our Lord and Saviour, Jesus Christ, to the occupants of the carriage.

"I DON'T REQUIRE AN APOLOGY"

A brother in the Lord once maliciously transgressed against him. A short time afterwards they appeared together on the same platform, apparently fast friends. An aged Christian, when conversing with my father later, inquired, "Did Mr. _____ apologize to you for his conduct, before you associated yourself with him?" "No, he didn't," he curtly replied, "What did I want with an apology? Wasn't it enough that he showed himself friendly towards me?"

SOME OF MR. REA'S FAVOURITE HYMNS

The following are some of his favourite hymns, which were largely sung at his meetings during specified periods of his ministry.

1869-1876

I hear the words of love;
    I gaze upon the blood;
I see the mighty sacrifice,
    And I have peace with God.

'Tis everlasting peace,
    Sure as Jehovah's name,
'Tis stable as His steadfast throne—
    For evermore the same.

The clouds may go and come,
    And storms may sweep my sky—
This blood-sealed friendship changes not,
    The cross is ever nigh.

My love is oft-times low,
    My joy still ebbs and flows;
But peace with Him remains the same,
    No change Jehovah knows.

I change—He changes not,
    My Christ can never die;
His love—not mine—the resting place;
    His truth—not mine—the tie.

Whene'er we meet, we always say,
   "What's the news?"
Pray, what's the order of the day?
   "What's the news?"
O I have got good news to tell:
My Saviour hath done all things well,
And triumphed over death and hell—
   That's the news.

The Lamb was slain on Calvary
To set a world of sinners free;
'Twas there His precious blood was shed,
'Twas there He bowed His sacred head,
But now He's risen from the dead—
   That's the news.

His work's reviving all around,
And many have redemption found;
And since their souls have caught the flame,
They shout Hosanna to His Name,
And all around they spread His fame—
   That's the news.

Poor sinner, Christ can save you now,
If lowly at His cross you bow;
This moment, if for sin you grieve,
This moment, if you will believe,
A full acquittal you'll receive—
   That's the news.

And then if any one should say,
    What's the news?
O tell them Christ has won the day,
That you have joined the conquering band,
And now with joy at God's command
You're marching to the better land—
    That's the news.

————

1877-1884

There were ninety and nine that safely lay
    In the shelter of the fold,
But one was out on the hills away,
    Far off from the gates of gold,
Away on the mountains wild and bare,
Away from the tender Shepherd's care.

"Lord, Thou hast here Thy ninety and nine,
    Are they not enough for Thee?"
But the Shepherd made answer, "This of Mine
    Has wandered away from Me;
And although the road be rough and steep,
I go to the desert to find My sheep."

But none of the ransomed ever knew
    How deep were the waters crossed,
Nor how dark was the night that the Lord
        passed thro',
    Ere He found His sheep that was lost.
Out in the desert He heard its cry,
Sick and helpless, and ready to die.

"Lord, whence are those blood-drops all the
      way,
   That mark out the mountain's track?"
"They were shed for one who had gone astray,
   Ere the Shepherd could bring him back."
"Lord, whence are Thy hands so rent and
      torn?"
"They are pierced tonight by many a thorn."

And all through the mountains, thunder-riven,
   And up from the rocky steep,
There arose a cry to the gate of heaven,—
   "Rejoice, I have found My sheep."
And the angels echoed around the throne,
"Rejoice, for the Lord brings back His own."

———

We have heard the wondrous tidings
   Of Thy grace in other climes,
And we pray that we may witness
   Similar refreshing times.

   Chorus –
   Lord revive us,
   Lord revive us,
   In our own beloved land.

We have heard how tents and barns
   Are with anxious sinners thronged;
How to Christ their hearts are yielding,
   Who to Satan once belonged.

We have heard how young and aged
   Deem their richest gain but loss;
How the wealthiest and the poorest
   Meet together at the Cross.

There are crowds of careless sinners
   Rushing to destruction's gate.
Come, Lord Jesus, come and stop them,
   Stop them ere it be too late.

———

We are going to Canaan's land,
   Never to come back any more,
To join the blood-bought, happy band,
   Never to come back any more.

Chorus:
Oh, no, no, no, no, never to come back any
   more,
No, no, no, no, never to come back any more.

When we go up the golden streets,
   Never to come back any more,
We'll ground our arms at Jesu's feet,
   Never to come back any more.

We have some friends gone on before,
   Never to come back any more,
We'll meet them singing on the shore,
   Never to come back any more.

We'll praise with yonder ransomed throng,
   Never to come back any more,
And join in the loud triumphant song,
   Never to come back any more.

O ye, who now salvation spurn,
   And will not enter Mercy's door,
Oh, dreadful thought, in Hell to burn,
   Never to come back any more.

———

1884-1890

I know there's a bright and a glorious land
   Away in the heaven's high,
Where all the redeemed shall with Jesus
      dwell—
   Will you be there and I?

In robes of white o'er the street of gold,
   Beneath a cloudless sky,
They'll walk in the light of their Father's
      love—
   Will you be there and I?

From every kingdom of earth they come
   To raises their anthems high;
Their harps will never be there unstrung—
   Will you be there and I?

If we trust the loving Saviour now,
   Who died on Calvary,
When He gathers His children in the bright
     home,
   Then you'll be there and I.

If we are sheltered by the Cross,
   And through the blood brought nigh,
Our utmost gain we'll count but loss,
   Since you'll be there and I.

———

Eternity! Time soon will end,
   Its fleeting moments pass away;
O sinner, say, where wilt thou spend
   Eternity's unchanging day?
  Shalt thou the hopeless horror see
  Of Hell for all eternity?

   Eternity! Eternity!
   Where wilt thou spend eternity?

Eternity! O dreadful thought
   For thee, a child of Adam's race,
If thou shouldst in thy sins be brought
   To stand before the awful face,
From which the heaven and earth shall flee,
   The Throned One of eternity.

Eternity! but Jesus died—
  Yes, Jesus died on Calvary;
Behold Him thorn-crowned, crucified,
  The spotless One made sin for thee;
O, sinner, haste: for refuge flee—
  He saves, and for eternity.

Eternity! behold the Lamb,
  Once slain, now lives, exalted high;
He calls thee, sinner, by thy name—
  Just as thou art to Him draw nigh;
Thy sins He bore to set thee free,
  Believe, and live eternally.

Tonight may be thy latest breath,
  Thy little moment here be done;
Eternal woe—the second death—
  Awaits the grace-rejecting one.
Thine awful destiny foresee—
  Time ends, and then Eternity!

1890-1896

From Salem's gates advancing slow
   What object meets mine eyes?
What means yon Majesty of woe?
   What mean those mingled cries?

Chorus:

O the blood of Jesus,
   The precious blood of Jesus;
O the blood of Jesus
   It cleanses from all sin.

Who can it be who groans beneath
   Yon ponderous cross of wood?
Whose soul's o'erwhelmed in fears of death,
   Whose body's bathed in blood?

Is this the Man? Can this be He
   The prophets have foretold
Should with transgressors numbered be,
   And for my crimes be sold?

Oh, lovely sight! Oh, heavenly form,
   For sinful souls to see!
I'll creep beside Him like a worm,
   And see Him die for me.

———

I was once far away from the Saviour,
  As vile as a sinner could be;
And I wondered if Christ, the Redeemer,
  Could save a poor sinner like me.

I wandered on in the darkness,
  Not a ray of light could I see;
And the thought filled my heart with sadness—
  There's no hope for a sinner like me.

And then in that dark, lonely hour,
  A voice sweetly whispered to me,
Saying, "Look unto Me: I have power
  To save a poor sinner like thee."

I listened, and lo! 'twas the Saviour
  That was speaking so kindly to me;
And I cried, "I'm the chief of all sinners;
  Canst Thou save a poor sinner like me?"

I then fully trusted in Jesus;
  And O, now a joy came to me:
My heart was filled with His praises
  For saving a sinner like me.

No longer in darkness I'm walking,
  The light is now shining on me;
And now unto others I'm telling
  How He saved a poor sinner like me.

And when life's journey is over,
  And I the dear Saviour shall see,
I'll praise Him for ever and ever
  For saving a sinner like me.

When my life-work is ended, and I cross the
    swelling tide,
    When the bright and glorious morning I
      shall see,
I shall know my Redeemer when I reach the
    other side,
    And His smile will be the first to welcome
      me.

Chorus:
I shall know Him, I shall know Him,
    When alone by His side I shall stand;
I shall know Him, I shall know Him,
    By the print of the nails in His hand.

O the soul-thrilling rapture when I view His
    blessed face,
    And the lustre of His kindly, beaming eye!
How my full heart will praise Him for His
    mercy, love and grace,
    That prepared for me a mansion in the sky!

O the dear ones in glory! How they beckon me
    to come!
    And our parting at the river I recall;
To the sweet vales of Eden they will sing my
    welcome home,
    But I long to see my Saviour first of all.

Thro' the gates of the city, in a robe of spotless
    white,
    He will lead me where no tears will ever fall;
In the glad song of ages I shall mingle with
    delight,
    But I long to meet my Saviour first of all.

1911-1916

There's a hill, lone and grey, in a land far
    away,
  In a country beyond the blue sea;
Where beneath that fair sky, went a Man forth
    to die,
  For the world, and for you and for me.

Chorus:

Oh, it bows down my heart, and the tear-drops
    will start,
  When in memory that grey hill I see;
For 'twas there, on its side, Jesus suffered and
    died,
  To redeem a poor sinner like me.

Behold, faint on the road, 'neath a world's
    heavy load,
  Comes a thorn-crowned man on the way;
With a cross He is bowed, but still on thro' the
    crowd
  He's ascending that hill lone and grey.

Hark! I hear the dull blow of the hammer,
    swung low;
  They are nailing my Lord to the tree;
And the cross they upraise, while the
    multitude gaze
  On the blest Lamb of dark Calvary.

How they mock Him in death, to His last
    lab'ring breath,
  While His friends sadly weep o'er the way;

But tho' lonely and faint, still no word of
    complaint
  Fell from Him on the hill lone and grey.

———

Have you read the story of the Cross,
  Where Jesus bled and died,
Where your debt was paid by His precious
    blood
  That flowed from His wounded side?

Have you read how they placed the crown of
    thorns
  Upon His lovely brow?—
When He prayed, "Forgive them, oh, forgive,
  They know not what they do."

Have you read how He saved the dying thief,
  When hanging on the tree?
Who looked with pitying eyes and said,
  "Dear Lord, remember me."

Have you heard that he looked to Heaven and
    said,
  " 'Tis finished" — it was for thee?
Have you ever said, "I thank Thee, Lord,
  For giving Thy life for me."

Chorus:
He died an atoning death for thee,
  He died an atoning death;
Oh, wondrous love! It was for thee
  He died an atoning death.

Chapter 27

HIS HOME LIFE

The preceding pages portray, in some measure, the character and energy of one who never wearied in the work which the Lord had called him to accomplish.

The numbers of Christians to be found throughout the length and breadth of the land, who have been led to the Saviour through his instrumentality, are, in themselves, abundant evidence of the Lord's approval of his ministry. Although often labouring under most trying circumstances, and with the care of a family of motherless children, he never wavered in going forth to proclaim the love of God.

My mother having pre-deceased him by twenty-eight years, domestic responsibilities and family obligations fell more heavily upon him than would have been the case had she lived; but the deep love which he had for his children enabled him to overcome many home difficulties.

For several years before his death, he devoted a great part of his time to physical labour, but this did not hinder him from attending to his work in the Gospel. Day after day he was to be found at his home in Sydenham, with coat off, and perspiration streaming from his brow, engaged in a work which he had undertaken, in order to discharge a certain voluntary obligation; and night after night he was to be seen at his tent, proclaiming the Gospel to the hundreds who assembled there.

No parent ever loved his children more than he did, and it was his great affection and godly, consistent home-life that caused me, when I was a wayward and rebellious sinner, to ponder on whither I was drifting. In those days I could withstand the entreaties of others who besought me to accept Christ as my Saviour, indeed, I could even scoff at the messengers of Grace; but my heart softened and the tears often came to my eyes when I thought of the love of my devoted father and of the unmerited kindness which he had so abundantly lavished upon me.

A WORD TO THE UNSAVED

The Apostle Paul so felt his responsibility towards God and man that he said: "Woe is unto me, if I preach not the Gospel" (1 Cor. 9:16), and again he says: "I am not ashamed of the Gospel of Christ, for it is the power of God unto salvation to every one that believeth" (Rom. 1:16).

There was no work in which my father more delighted than the preaching of the Gospel, either from a public platform, or by personal conversation with his fellow-travellers to eternity; and he often said that nothing gave him greater joy than to know that he had been used of God in leading sinners to the Saviour.

Knowing, as I do, what was the aim and object of his life, it would not be fitting that I should conclude without devoting a portion of this work exclusively to the pointing of my unsaved readers to "the Lamb of God, which taketh away the sin of the world."

The Lord Himself, in replying to the enquiries of a religious Jewish leader, one well versed in the law, says plainly, in no uncertain language, "Except a man be born again, he cannot see the Kingdom of God."

To the Philippian jailor, who had thrust the servants of the living God into prison, after they had been illegally flogged, Paul said, "Believe on the Lord Jesus Christ and thou shalt be saved." The Apostle Peter, too, on the Day of Pentecost, in addressing the multitude (many of whom had been amongst those who, when asked to choose between Jesus and the malefactor, Barabbas, had cried, "Away with Him, away with Him, Crucify Him, and release unto us Barabbas"), after charging them with having murdered the Son of God, in almost the same breath breaks forth with the words, "Repent and be baptised every one of you, in the name of Jesus Christ, for the remission of sins, and ye shall receive the gift of the Holy Ghost."

Thus we see the grace of God reaching out to all types of sinners: to a religious leader, to a hardened jailor, and to a blood-thirsty mob, who had clamoured for the crucifixion of their best Friend.

Are you a church-going member, upright as a Cornelius, zealous for your church as a Saul of Tarsus, but unconverted? Then I would point you to the One who said, "Verily, verily, I say unto you, 'YE MUST BE BORN AGAIN' " — the One Who bore your sins in His own body on the tree, that you might inherit eternal life. "For as Moses lifted up the serpent in the wilderness, even so must the Son

of Man be lifted up." Ah, religious sinner, God in
His word says, "All your righteousness is as filthy
rags," and "By grace are ye saved through faith, and
that not of yourselves, it is the gift of God. Not of
works lest any man should boast." I would now
beseech you, in the language of the hymn, to

> "Cast your deadly doing down,
>   Down at Jesu's feet,
> Stand in Him, in Him, alone,
>   Gloriously complete."

Are you a hardened and careless sinner? Then I
implore you to stop and think before you go
further, for the time will come when you must bow
the knee to Jesus and confess Him as Lord, to the
Glory of God the Father. You must meet Him either
as your Saviour or your Judge.

The message of Paul and Silas to the convicted
jailor who fell trembling at their feet was, "Believe
on the Lord Jesus Christ and thou shalt be saved."
"And they spake unto him the word of God" (Acts
16:31, 32.)

Methinks that they would point out to this jailor
that the Jesus whom they preached was the One to
whom Isaiah of old had referred, when he said: "He
was wounded for our transgressions, He was
bruised for our iniquities; the chastisement of our
peace was upon Him, and with His stripes we are
healed," and that it was He Who was crucified at
Jerusalem between two malefactors, buried in
Joseph of Arimathæa's new tomb, and on the third
day triumphantly arose from the dead; and that it

was He Who, forty days later, in the presence of His followers, ascended from Mount Olivet to heaven: and as the clouds received Him out of their sight, two men stood by them in white apparel, and said: "Ye men of Galilee, why stand ye gazing up into heaven? This same Jesus, which is taken up from you into heaven, shall so come in like manner as ye have seen Him go into heaven" (Acts 1:11). The Philippian jailor, hardened sinner as he was, accepted the Lord Jesus Christ, and was saved.

Now, dear unsaved reader, will you, like this jailor, take Christ as your Saviour, and rejoice, as he did, in the knowledge of sins forgiven?

No matter how deeply you have sunk in sin, the grace of God can reach you, for the Scripture saith: "He came not to call the righteous, but sinners to repentance," and, "Though your sins be as scarlet, they shall be as white as snow, though they be red like crimson, they shall be as wool," and, "The blood of Jesus Christ, His Son, cleanseth us from all sin." Do not trifle any longer with the question of your soul's salvation. Get the matter settled at once. The issues are too vastly important to permit of delay. The eternal welfare of your soul is at stake. A glorious Heaven, with Christ its centre of attraction and admiration, awaits you if you put your trust in Him; but if you neglect this great salvation, what then? — banishment from God. Oh, the miseries, oh, the woes, oh, the agonies, which will be the lot of the Christ-rejector! Can you bear the thought of being consigned to an endless Hell, to suffer torment where the "worm dieth not, and the fire is not quenched?" Do not procrastinate. Christ is waiting to save you now.

> "The Spirit and the Bride say 'Come',
>   Oh, sinner, haste, from wrath to flee.
> An hour's delay may seal your doom,
>   Don't trifle with ETERNITY."

"For God so loved the world, that He gave His only begotten Son, that whosoever believeth in Him should not perish, but have everlasting life."

Chapter 28

HOME-CALL OF MY MOTHER

On pages 82 to 84 of this book will be found the story of the conversion and home-call of my my father brother, William Henry, as recorded byin his manuscripts. Before I conclude, however, I should like also to relate some of the cirumstances respecting the "departure to be with Christ" of my mother, and of my sisters, Henrietta and Rachel.

No more loving and devoted wife, nor more affectionate parent than my mother ever lived. She was a most exemplary Christian. I have still fresh recollections of how she gathered us around her, in the absence of my father, and read and prayed with us, and of how fervently she besought God to bless father in his work in the Gospel. She shared his joys with unspeakable delight, and when adversity overtook us in our home-life, it was she who encouraged him to continue to look to the Lord for help in time of trouble.

How often have I seen her radiant expression of joy on the day that my father was expected home, as she eagerly watched for the train, which passed near our house, and for a glimpse of the handkerchief, which he invariably waved as the train passed by. But the Lord in His grace saw it good to take her to Himself when I was a mere lad.

She was confined to bed for a considerable time before her death, but she bore her sufferings without a murmur, and as it came nearer the end, her joy increased. She often said, "What a glorious home-call it will be!"

On the afternoon of the day of her "departure," the doctor, on entering the room, said to her, "Well, Mrs. Rea, how have you got the day in?" "I have just been waiting all the day for the 'Glory.' Oh, doctor, it's blessed to have Christ!" she replied, and repeated the following lines:—

> "Content to go, content to stay,
>   Content to suffer still;
> Content to glory in the Cross,
>   And wait His blessed will."

As my father stood by her bedside weeping, she said to him, "Why are you sad, David? Why are you not praising God? Do praise Him."

When asked if there were any particular hymns that she would like sung at her funeral, she replied, "Praise the Lord in the most joyful hymns, and thank Him for having taken me to Himself."

She fell asleep in Jesus that same evening, the 11th of August, 1888, at the age of 51 years.

> Gone for a robe of spotless white,
> Gone into Heaven's unsullied light,
> Gone where they see the Saviour's face,
> Gone as a trophy of saving grace,
> Gone where the storms for ever cease,
> Gone into Heaven's unruffled peace,
> Gone from sorrow, in patience borne,
> Gone where it is one eternal morn!

HENRIETTA

Henrietta, who departed to be with Christ in February, 1892, at the age of 16½ years, was the next of our family to be called "up higher." I can best tell her story in the words of the little booklet, written by my father, which has been largely circulated and eagerly read during the past few years:—

HENRIETTA'S LAST WORDS:

("I'm going in.")

WRITTEN BY MY FATHER

Henrietta Rea was brought to a saving knowledge of Christ in the month of July, 1887, being at that time about twelve years of age. She and the other children had for a long time been the subject of much prayer. I often felt in deep anxiety and sore distress about their salvation, and frequently spoke to them of the danger in putting off and rejecting Christ. A few Christian friends came from Glasgow to spend a short time with us. They had a deep love for souls, and were not long with us ere I felt sure that blessing was nigh; but it far exceeded my expectations. Mrs. L____, one of the friends, took a special interest in the girls, and night and day essing kept pron them the importance of eternal things, so that very soon deep conviction of sin took hold of them. I cannot describe the joy that filled my heart one night as I returned home from tent work. My eldest daughter met me at the door, and told me that she had found peace in Christ during the afternoon of that day. How we praised and thanked the Lord till a late hour that night for His mercy in saving her! but about one o'clock next morning we were aroused from sleep by dear Hennie and her sister (two years older) rushing into our bedroom and telling us they had just been saved. This was more than we were prepared for; the news was so good we could hardly believe it, but time proved it to be a blessed reality, as up to February, 1892, dear Henrietta bore a bright testimony to the grace that saved and kept her. To God and the Lamb be all glory.

She told me afterwards that long before she was converted, when going to the meetings, she often trembled lest she should cry out before the people. How many, like dear Henrietta, especially in youth, stifle conviction and check the falling tear! She showed a remarkable amount of intelligence, far beyond her years, and was most conscientious in all her ways. Having lost her mother twelve months or so after her conversion, she showed great care for both the spiritual and temporal welfare of her brother and sisters. All who came in contact with her, whether at school or other places, were drawn to her, her winning ways being natural and unaffected. But her time for testimony on earth was very short, as, three years after her conversion, symptoms of consumption made their appearance, and, notwithstanding all the efforts to check its progress, it went on and increased until all hope of recovery was given up.

Whilst on a visit to a watering-place at the end of the season the Lord's presence was again mightily manifested on a Saturday night in the salvation of

THE LAST TWO OF OUR FAMILY

It was a touching sight to see her on her knees, pointing her little sister, ten years of age, who was in deep soul distress, to the Saviour; and then leading aloud in prayer and thanksgiving after the little one had found peace.

After this, she had about four months of increased bodily weakness, and at times intense suffering; but it was most blessed to hear her, even in the depths of her weakness and pain, praising God, and rejoicing in the knowledge of sins forgiven, and in the blessed hope of soon being with Christ for ever. Sometimes for hours she would be in raptures of joy, and the sweet, happy expression of her face was indescribable. She said to me on one occasion, "Oh, father, won't it be blessed to see the Lamb, and be with Him on His throne! — and then the angels about the throne!" I said to her on another occasion, "Won't it be nice, Hennie, to meet your mother and brother already gone before?" "Ah," said she, "I am not thinking so much about my mother; it is Christ I want to see, the One who died for me."

Her weakness was so great that at times she could not see her own sisters, and about three weeks before her departure, she was severely tried by nervous spasms. The last one was most pitiful to witness. I was sitting behind her in the bed, endeavouring to afford her some relief, and when she was at the worst, I said to her, "Dear Hennie, do think of the precious Lord Jesus, who poured out His life's blood on the Cross for you." In a second there was perfect calm, and all the pain was gone. She then turned round and kissed me, and praised God. She had no return of the agony. O the power of the precious Name of Jesus! Before it all pain and diseases must flee, as in the days of His flesh.

Sometimes, during the night, she would call to me and say, "Father, I am very happy; do you think I might get home tonight?" As long as she was able to bear it, she would ask me to read her regular portions of God's Word, and then would say, "Oh, how refreshing His Word is!" And when she could no longer bear it, she would ask me to quote her a passage slowly, or the first line of a hymn.

SIX DAYS BEFORE HER END...

...she had a remarkable manifestation of the presence of God, and a glorious foretaste of heaven. For hours she lay basking in God's light on the verge of glory, expecting every moment to enter in. The expression of her face was simply beautiful, and it was grand to hear her as she said, "The gates seem to be a little ajar; but I cannot enter yet. O if only you felt what I now feel, and saw what I now see!" Then another burst of praise to the Lord Jesus — "It is all through His blood, His precious blood; won't you tell the doctor that I am gone to glory?" The doctor, being a true Christian, helped her much spiritually as well as bodily. I tried to feel her pulse,

but she said, "Don't mind, father, I want it to stop."
To Mr. Bell, a valued friend, who with his wife and
daughter came to visit her at that time, she said,
"Mr. Bell, you have been preaching the Gospel for a
long time, and my father has been preaching a good
while too; but you have NEVER HALF TOLD the love
of Christ." Then she said to him, "I want you, Mr.
Stewart, and Mr. McLean to preach at my funeral,
and warn the people, as I did not warn them as I
should have done when in health. (She often
grieved over her unfaithfulness.) I would like you to
put bills up through the town to warn the people,
and you could give one to J.M. to put in his window,
if he has the heart to do it."

The following night was also one of

REMARKABLE SOUL ECSTASY.

As long as she could hold them up, she kept
clapping her hands, and shouting, "Hallelujah,
Glory to God!" and commenced singing the hymn,
"O Christ, in Thee my soul hath found." She then
asked me to remind her of another, as she could not
remember. So I gave her the hymn, "I have a song I
love to sing, since I have been redeemed." She
finished up with, "They are gathering homeward
from every land." And looking at her elder sister,
she said, "M.A., stand fast for Jesus, and tell father
everything, as he knows better than you."

Next day she arranged all about her funeral, and
told me what she had done with her clothes and
other little things, and then with a sigh, she said,
"Father, I have nothing for you." To a sister who
helped to nurse her she said, "I have no more

longing now for food; I long now for Home." Next morning at three o'clock she called me to her, and said, "Father, are you rejoicing?" But with so much sitting up I felt in a stupor, and hardly knew what to say. I asked her how she felt herself. "I am very happy," she replied. On the Tuesday before her departure, while Mr. Kingston (another warm friend, who was with her to the end), was helping to settle her pillows, she said, "Do you think I'll see Him today?" "No, dear Hennie," he replied, "it may be a day or two yet before you get Home." The doctor called the same day, and said to her, "Hennie, you are very weary?" "Yes, doctor," she answered, "but it will soon be rest."

On Thursday, which was her last day on earth, while standing beside her, I said, "Poor Hennie."

"RICH HENNIE,"

she replied. I then said, "Hennie, you will soon see the King in His beauty." She smiled, and her face lighted up with joy as she said, "O, it will be glorious." After a little while, "I think I'll be in by one," she said; and when it came to one, she asked what time it was, and when told ten minutes to one, she shouted, "Glory," but she did not get in then. I repeated to her the following lines, which so fully expressed her desire:—

"My thirsty spirit faints to reach the land I
    love—
The bright inheritance of saints, Jerusalem
    above."

The pain was so great, and still increasing, that she said, "O pray the Lord to take me now." Mr. Kingston and I kept praying for over half an hour, and when either of us stopped, she said, "O pray on, pray on." At one time she broke out in prayer herself (and how she did emphasise the endearing Name!) — "O Father, do give me patience to wait Thy time." She then beckoned to me to speak to her, and when I put down my head to hear what she had to say, she said, "Deliverance has come." "Thank the Lord," said Mr. Kingston, "for sending you relief from pain." "O no," said she, "it is not that —

I AM GOING IN."

And in a few minutes she breathed her last on earth, and passed into the presence of the King!

The following words, quoted by Mr. Bell at the grave, were very appropriate:—

"I kissed the nail-holes in His hands,
    And where the spear went in;
I make His Cross my sure retreat
    From all the storms of sin;
The napkin that He left behind
    Has wiped my weeping eyes,
And I in His own bosom find
    My lasting Paradise."

Her funeral was carried out in full accordance with her wishes. The meeting at the house was large, mostly composed of Christians from many parts. It was opened by Mr. Stewart, who gave out the hymn— "Once more, my soul, Thy Saviour

through the Word," and, after a solemn time of
prayer, he read the striking narrative in Luke 16,
verse 19 to the end, of the death and eternal destiny
of two men — the rich man and Lazarus. He first
spoke to those who were in Christ and who
consequently knew their sins forgiven, of the
solemn responsibility, of the importance of being
wholly consecrated to the Lord, and filling up the
precious moments between this time and His
coming again.

He then addressed the unsaved upon the awful
consequences of putting off salvation to a dying
hour, or even of harbouring such a thought as that
any change could take place in Eternity, referring to
the two requests of the rich man in Hell:— first,
that Lazarus might be sent to "Dip the tip of his
finger in the water, and cool my tongue, for I am
tormented in this flame"; secondly, on this being
denied him, that Lazarus might be sent to his five
brethren, who were still on earth, to warn them
"that they come not into this place of torment."
Then he showed how he was answered with the
words, "They have Moses and the prophets; neither
will they be persuaded, though one rose from the
dead." It was a very heart-searching time. Mr. Bell
then followed with the hymn —

"Eternity—time soon will end."

After reading John 5:24 to 29, he very touchingly
referred to

THE BRIGHT TESTIMONY

of the departed one. He then showed God's beautiful order in salvation from the words, "Verily, verily, I say unto you, he that HEARETH My Word, and BELIEVETH on Him that sent Me, HATH everlasting life." First, HEARING; secondly, BELIEVING; and next, HAVING, that is, being in present possession of everlasting life, and the ETERNAL SECURITY of such. He briefly referred in verse 29 to the resurrection of the just and the unjust; one to life, and the other to damnation:—nothing between, no medium class or destiny. He concluded by reference to 1 Thess. 4:14 to the end, where the Spirit, by the Apostle, brings before the saints the blessed, reviving, and comforting hope of the SOON COMING LORD, to raise up the sleeping ones, to change the living, and to call them up

TO MEET HIMSELF IN THE AIR,

so to be "for ever with the Lord," dwelling particularly on the words, "The Lord HIMSELF shall descend" (not send Gabriel, nor millions of angels, but come HIMSELF).

The hymn was then sung—

"For ever with the Lord."

About the appointed time, the funeral procession started, singing the hymn— "I have a song I love to sing." Other suitable hymns were sung on the way to the grave.

At the grave Mr. McLean gave out the hymn,

"The Gospel of Thy Grace, my stubborn heart has won." He then spoke from the words, "Precious in the sight of the Lord is the death of His saints" (Psalm 116:15). He very forcibly contrasted it with Ezekiel 18:23, and 33:11, where God says, "Have I any pleasure at all that the wicked should die? As I live, saith the Lord God, I have no pleasure in the death of the wicked. Turn ye, turn ye from your evil ways, for WHY WILL YE DIE?" He pointedly and solemnly pressed this truth home upon the unsaved. A solemn awe pervaded the whole place, and all present seemed to feel the power of the Word. After prayer and the singing of the hymn, "The blast of the trumpet," dear Henrietta's remains were committed to the dust, till that day, "When this corruptible shall have put on incorruption, and this mortal shall have put on immortality, and death shall be swallowed up in victory." "O death, where is thy sting? O grave, where is thy victory? The sting of death is sin; and the strength of sin is the law. But thanks be to God, which giveth us the

VICTORY THROUGH OUR LORD JESUS CHRIST."

RACHEL

My sister, Rachel, fell asleep in Jesus on the 22nd July, 1894, at the age of twenty years. She, too, had an abundant entrance into the Kingdom.

Henrietta and she were converted on the same

night, in the month of July, 1887. The story of her
conversion is recorded by my father, and will be
found on page 111 of this book.

She dearly loved father, and took a great interest
in his work. The following are extracts from some
of her letters to him while he was labouring in
Aberdeen, in the early part of the year 1894:—

January 30th, 1894

"I am glad to hear of the marvellous power in the
work of the Lord; trusting that many hundreds may
be brought to Christ, and know their sins forgiven.

Mr. B. has gone this morning, so we are all alone
now, and it is very lonely sometimes; but I trust we
can deny ourselves that much for the Lord during
our short stay here; somehow I have a feeling in
myself that tells me it won't be long.

I hope you are still keeping up in body; I've been
dreaming about your being very ill, and coming
home."

February 5th, 1894

"Very glad to hear of the blessing of God being so
mightily manifest in the conversion of lost souls.
May the Lord continue to work. It will be very hard
for you to leave that place.

The Lord is very good to us in supplying our
wants; but how ungrateful we are to Him, and
undeserving of them."

February 7th, 1894

"Glad to hear that you are well; also that there are
some always passing from death unto life. I trust

your leaving will do the work no harm, and that Satan won't take advantage to close the door."

February 9th, 1894

"Glad to hear that the numbers are still increasing and the interest keeping up. I judge from your letters that Friday night will be the last week-night meeting; may it be very blessed, being the last."

HER LAST LETTER TO LONDON

April 30th, 1894

"I suppose this is my last letter — I can hardly write it, the time is so near. I am almost ready to watch for you; I will see you very soon — only two days. Thank the Lord for preserving us so far, and He will continue to do so until the end. Why should we ever doubt Him?"

A FEW OF HER LAST WORDS

After one of her severe, trying turns, while my father was mentioning the blood of Jesus, "Oh," she said, "how sweet the blood sounds in my ears! The more I think of it the firmer I feel; sometimes I have to cease thinking, afraid of getting too excited." Truly, Christ and eternal things were thrilling facts to her.

At the same time, reaching out her hand and shutting it, she said to Mrs. B., "If I had anything in that hand, wouldn't I be sure of it?" "Yes," said Mrs. B., "you would." "Well, that is just how I feel about Heaven; I feel so certain of it."

The evening before her departure, when we thought she was nearly gone, my father repeated the words of Samuel Rutherford, "Lovely Jesus," she smiled, and said, "Oh, how sweet it will be to see Him!" Her hands getting cold, she looked up and said to father, "Aren't my hands getting cold?" "Yes, Rachel," he said. Her face brightened, she shook her head, and said, "Isn't that good?"

She felt much disappointed in not getting away that evening. The next morning, which was her last on earth, my father said to her, "When in prayer this morning and asking the Lord about you, the thought struck me that He had given you another day to witness for Him." "I was just thinking about that myself, and if I could only speak a word for the Lord," she replied. And truly the Lord gave her her desire; for, about two hours before the close, a friend, whom she highly esteemed for uprightness, came in to see her, to whom she said with great earnestness, "One thing thou lackest." The friend, misunderstanding her, said, "Oh, anything you request me to do, I will do it." "Oh it's not that," she said, "don't you know that passage in God's Word? It's your salvation I mean. I shall soon be in Heaven, and I want you to meet me there." Afterwards looking at a relation who had professed conversion, but had fallen back, she said, "I haven't long to be here now, and I'm sorry I've seen no signs of repentance yet in you." He left the room, shut himself up, confessed his sin, and has since professed restoration.

Shortly after, the doctor came in and said all would soon be over. "Thank the Lord," she said; and in a few minutes she was with the One she loved.

AT HOME WITH THE LORD

No more faint journeyings weary,
No more the storm-clouds dreary,
No more on earth the cross to bear,
But now with Christ a crown to wear;
No more faint journeyings weary,—
   Now with Christ at home.

No more the sound of weeping,
No more night-watches keeping,
No more conflicts now with sin,
No more lost souls for Christ to win;
No more faint journeyings weary,—
   Now with Christ at home.

No more sweet ties to sever,
No more sad words for ever,
No more sad partings on the strand,
The Jordan crossed—in Canaan's land!
No more faint journeyings weary,—
   Now with Christ at home.

THE END